THIS I
BELIEVE

Previous books published by John Wiley & Sons in the *This I Believe* series, edited by Dan Gediman, John Gregory, and Mary Jo Gediman:

This I Believe: On Love

This I Believe: On Fatherhood

THIS I BELIEVE

Life Lessons

EDITED BY DAN GEDIMAN
WITH JOHN GREGORY
AND MARY JO GEDIMAN

John Wiley & Sons, Inc.

This book is printed on acid-free paper. ∞

Copyright © 2011 by This I Believe, Inc. All rights reserved.

This I Believe® is a registered trademark of This I Believe, Inc.

Published by John Wiley & Sons, Inc., Hoboken, New Jersey
Published simultaneously in Canada

Design by Forty-five Degree Design LLC

No part of this publication may be reproduced, stored in a retrieval system, or transmitted in any form or by any means, electronic, mechanical, photocopying, recording, scanning, or otherwise, except as permitted under Section 107 or 108 of the 1976 United States Copyright Act, without either the prior written permission of the Publisher, or authorization through payment of the appropriate per-copy fee to the Copyright Clearance Center, 222 Rosewood Drive, Danvers, MA 01923, (978) 750-8400, fax (978) 646-8600, or on the web at www.copyright.com. Requests to the Publisher for permission should be addressed to the Permissions Department, John Wiley & Sons, Inc., 111 River Street, Hoboken, NJ 07030, (201) 748-6011, fax (201) 748-6008, or online at http://www.wiley.com/go/permissions.

Limit of Liability/Disclaimer of Warranty: While the publisher and the author have used their best efforts in preparing this book, they make no representations or warranties with respect to the accuracy or completeness of the contents of this book and specifically disclaim any implied warranties of merchantability or fitness for a particular purpose. No warranty may be created or extended by sales representatives or written sales materials. The advice and strategies contained herein may not be suitable for your situation. You should consult with a professional where appropriate. Neither the publisher nor the author shall be liable for any loss of profit or any other commercial damages, including but not limited to special, incidental, consequential, or other damages.

For general information about our other products and services, please contact our Customer Care Department within the United States at (800) 762-2974, outside the United States at (317) 572-3993, or fax (317) 572-4002.

Wiley also publishes its books in a variety of electronic formats and by print-on-demand. Some content that appears in standard print versions of this book may not be available in other formats. For more information about Wiley products, visit us at www.wiley.com.

Library of Congress Cataloging-in-Publication Data:
    This I believe : life lessons / edited by Dan Gediman with Mary Jo Gediman and John Gregory. — 1st ed.
        p. cm.
    ISBN 978-1-118-07454-1 (cloth); 978-1-118-48199-8 (paper);
    ISBN 978-1-118-09740-3 (ebk); ISBN 978-1-118-09742-7 (ebk);
    ISBN 978-1-118-09743-4 (ebk)
        1. Life. 2. Conduct of life. I. Gediman, Dan. II. Gediman, Mary Jo.
III. Gregory, John, 1964-
BD431.T287   2011
170'.44—dc23

                                                                        2011024778

Printed in the United States of America
10 9 8 7 6 5

To Margot Trevor Wheelock,
who was responsible for
This I Believe

CONTENTS

Introduction

In the early 1950s, prominent American newsman Edward R. Murrow and three colleagues came up with a novel idea: to ask individuals to write their own personal credo, a story of the rules by which they lived, in six hundred words or less. Then they asked each person to share that philosophy for living by reading his or her essay aloud on national radio. The reason was simple: at a time of uncertainty about the future, when matters of belief divided our country and the world, Murrow felt that broadcasting a daily personal reflection on one's guiding principles would help listeners find answers to their own questions about living.

At its foundation, writing a *This I Believe* essay is about declaring one's own personal philosophy of life by telling a story about how those beliefs were formed. When people strip down their beliefs to their core principles, they might find that the longest-lasting beliefs are those based on a moment when something they have learned stays with them forever.

A life lesson is one of those defining moments—a moment that teaches us something that we remember and carry forward. A life lesson, and the story behind it, is something we feel has altered us, great or slight, and after that moment we are changed. A simple observation becomes a beacon that offers guidance, direction, or meaning—and a foundation for living.

The world's religions, of course, have stories of life lessons at their core—love your neighbor, treat others as you wish to be treated, know thyself. And we also glean instructions for living through classic children's fairy tales and folklore handed down through generations. Even movies and video games of today teach us that taking risks is the only way to get ahead and perseverance is a virtue.

So life lessons don't necessarily have to be *lived* in order to be *learned.* Reading or listening to the life lessons of others can give us insight into their experiences, and we may reflect on how we might integrate that wisdom into our own lives. Indeed, we have heard from many people over the years who have told us that after listening to a *This I Believe* essay on the radio or reading one in a book, they find they believe that, too, and it alters or augments their own personal credo.

Although some of these stories are certainly different from your own experience, there may be a life lesson at the core that will resonate inside. You may not be a roller derby queen or a physician, a corporate executive, or a homeless person, but you might just find you have something you can learn from their stories.

In this book, you'll find ponderings on life's big questions, such as "Why am I here?" and "What is my place in the world?" There are beliefs in the importance of saying hello, saying thank-you, and saying "I forgive you." And there are revelations on the importance of listening to your inner voice and taking responsibility for your actions.

Some writers tell stories of making lemonade out of lemons, loving one's enemies, and putting beliefs into action. There are also lessons on the kindness of strangers, neighbors, and friends. And there are reflections on the resiliency of people—living through cancer, depression, or an accident and coming through it with their spirits not only intact but perhaps even stronger and more enriched as a result of what they experienced.

In this collection, you'll also find that wisdom isn't always a product of age. Some essays are written by those with several decades of life experience, while others have been written by teenagers. While older writers tell of lessons learned and tested throughout a lifetime, younger writers speak from a newly forged, and equally powerful, perspective.

This book is for the bedside table or the student's backpack. It might be read a little bit every day, or all at once. Either way, we hope it will be read over and over, with dog-eared pages and notes in the margins. And we hope that you, after reading it, will be moved to write your own statement of belief.

The Power of Hello

HOWARD WHITE

I work at a company where there are about a gazillion employees. I can't say that I know them all by name, but I know my fair share of them. I think that almost all of them know me. I'd say that's the reason I've been able to go wherever it is I've made it to in this world. It's all based on one simple principle: I believe that every single person deserves to be acknowledged, however small or simple the greeting.

When I was about ten years old, I was walking down the street with my mother. She stopped to speak to Mr. Lee. I was busy trying to bull's-eye the O on the stop sign with a rock. I knew I could see Mr. Lee any old time around the neighborhood, so I didn't pay any attention to him. After we passed Mr. Lee, my mother stopped me and said something that has stuck with me from that day until now. She said, "You let that be the last time you ever walk by somebody and not open up your mouth to speak, because even a dog can wag its tail when it passes you on the street." That phrase sounds simple, but it's been a guidepost for me and the foundation of who I am.

When you write an essay like this, you look in the mirror and see who you are and what makes up your character. I realized mine was cemented that day when I was ten years old. Even then, I started to see that when I spoke to someone, they spoke back. And that felt good.

It's not just something I believe in; it's become a way of life. I believe that every person deserves to feel someone acknowledge their presence, no matter how humble they may be or even how important.

At work, I always used to say hello to the founder of the company and ask him how our business was doing. But I also spoke to the people in the café and the people who cleaned the buildings and asked how their children were doing. After a few years of passing by the founder, I had the courage to ask him for a meeting. We had a great talk. At a certain point I asked him how far he thought I could go in his company. He said, "If you want to, you can get all the way to this seat."

I've become vice president, but that hasn't changed the way I approach people. I still follow my mother's advice. I speak to everyone I see, no matter where I am. I've learned that speaking to people creates a pathway into their world, and it lets them come into mine, too.

The day you speak to someone who has their head down but lifts it up and smiles, you realize how powerful it is just to open your mouth and say, "Hello."

Former University of Maryland point guard HOWARD WHITE is vice president of Jordan Brand at Nike. He founded Believe to Achieve, Nike's motivational program for youth, and he wrote a book by the same name. Mr. White lives with his wife, Donna, and his daughter, Mandy, in Lake Oswego, Oregon. He is proud to note that Mandy is a two-time All American at the University of Oregon.

The Art of Being a Neighbor

EVE BIRCH

I used to believe in the American Dream, which meant a job, a mortgage, cable TV, credit cards, warranties, success. I wanted it and worked toward it like everyone else, all of us separately chasing the same thing.

One year, through a series of unhappy events, it all fell apart. I found myself homeless and alone. I had my truck and $56.

I scoured the countryside for some place I could rent for the cheapest possible amount. I came upon a shack in an isolated hollow four miles up a winding mountain road over the Potomac River in West Virginia.

It was abandoned, full of broken glass and rubbish. When I pried off the plywood over a window and climbed in, I found something I could put my hands to. I hadn't been alone for twenty-five years. I was scared, but I hoped the hard work would distract and heal me.

I found the owner and rented the place for $50 a month. I took a bedroll, a broom, a rope, a gun, and some cooking gear, and I cleared a corner to camp in while I worked.

The locals knew nothing about me. But slowly, they started teaching me the art of being a neighbor. They dropped off blankets, candles, tools, and canned deer meat, and they began sticking around to chat. They asked if I wanted to meet cousin Albie or go fishing, maybe get drunk some night. They started to teach me a belief in a different American Dream—not the one of individual achievement but of neighborliness.

Men would stop by with wild berries, ice cream, truck parts, and bullets to see if I was up for courting. I wasn't, but they were civil anyway. The women on that mountain worked harder than any I'd ever met. They taught me how to use a whetstone to sharpen my knives, how to store food in the creek, and how to keep it cold and safe. I learned to keep enough food for an extra plate for company.

What I had believed in, all those things I thought were the necessary accoutrements for a civilized life, were nonexistent in this place. Up on the mountain, my most valuable possessions were my relationships with my neighbors.

After four years in that hollow, I moved back into town. I saw that a lot of people were having a really hard time, losing their jobs and homes. With the help of a real estate broker I chatted up at the grocery store, I managed to rent a big enough house to take in a handful of people.

There are four of us now in the house, but over time I've had nine people come in and move on to other places from here. We'd all be in shelters if we hadn't banded together.

The American Dream I believe in now is a shared one. It's not so much about what I can get for myself; it's about how we can all get by together.

EVE BIRCH is a librarian in Martinsburg, West Virginia, where she still works with the homeless while also running a small construction business that provides day work for needy neighbors. Two stories Ms. Birch wrote about her life in the shack are featured in the anthology *The Green Rolling Hills*.

A Kind and Generous Heart

CHRISTINE LITTLE

I learned my belief from my son. I believe in selfless giving.

Eight years ago, my thirteen-year-old son, Dustin, became very ill with a heart enlarged to double its size. The medical term, as unimportant as that is to a grieving mother, was cardiomyopathy. For several months Dustin lived on life support as we were forced to stand by and watch him wither away. While his friends were out playing baseball, flirting with girls, and sleeping in their own beds, my son was in a hospital bed, attached to a machine that kept his heart beating. As a mother, my first reaction after crying was anger, and then I played the bargaining game: "Take my life for his, Lord. I've lived my life, but he still has so much to do."

People all around me were praying for a heart to become available, but it made me so angry and confused because I knew for that to happen, someone else's child would have to die. How could anyone pray for that?

I still remember so clearly the morning we got the call that there was a heart. As we stood in Dustin's hospital room watching them prep him for surgery, we experienced the true definition of bittersweet. His dad and I, seemingly in unison, realized that at the precise moment that we were standing there with so much hope and so much love, another family somewhere was saying good-bye. We knelt down together and cried, and we prayed for them and thanked them for giving such a selfless gift.

To our amazement, just ten days later, Dustin got to come home for the first time in many months. He had turned fourteen in the hospital, and at such a young age he had received a second chance at life. Over the next two years he got to go to high school, learn to drive, and have his first girlfriend. He got to spend time with his family and be in the great outdoors, which was where he truly loved to be. He put his brand new heart to good use volunteering at the homeless shelter and helping the elderly. He also became a very devoted Christian young man.

Dustin's new heart failed him when he was sixteen. A tragedy, yes, but we have to see it as the miracle it was. We received two precious years with him that we would never have had without organ donation. We have more pictures, more memories, and a great satisfaction in knowing that he was able to experience some of the most exciting times and milestones in a teenager's life.

When he died, as difficult as it was for us, we knew that it would be Dustin's wish to give back. His eyes went to someone who wanted to see. Someone who, perhaps, had never seen the faces of the family they loved so dearly. I believe that one day I will look into the face of someone else's son or daughter and I will see those sky-blue eyes looking back at me—the evidence of selfless giving.

CHRISTINE LITTLE is a circulation clerk at the public library in Bettendorf, Iowa, where she lives with her three other children, a dog, a cat, and a very mouthy parrotlet. In her spare time, Ms. Little enjoys reading, writing, and relaxing on the beach with her family.

Make It Do

∾

PATRICIA ANDERSON

The simple life I live comes easy for me. It's a family tradition. I remember listening, as a small child, to stories my parents told of surviving the Great Depression—tales of the deprivations they endured and the sacrifices the family made. My father was lucky to have a job, but he walked twenty-six blocks from his home to his office to save a nickel in carfare. My mother stopped putting sugar in her coffee, and she learned to cook without meat. My sister wore mended clothes to high school. And they say my grandmother counted the lumps of coal put into the furnace each day. It was a time of staying close to home and learning to live with what you already had and being thankful for whatever that might be.

When I was growing up in another time of economic hardship, World War II, there were more sacrifices to be made. My father went for years without a new suit. Mother still had no sugar for her coffee, and we were, by then, vegetarians. My sister went without nylons, and I wore hand-me-downs to elementary school. We had no tires for the car. And so, once again, we stayed close to home and "made do." It seemed the lessons of the Great Depression served us well during wartime. And they serve me well today.

My mother made a little painted plaque to hang in our kitchen that spelled out this philosophy for living. It hung right above the drawer where we saved string and tinfoil.

> Use it up.
> Wear it out.
> Make it do.
> Or do without.

This is how I live. Today I have a small mobile home with a tiny yard. I cut the grass with a rotary mower, and I grow vegetables in a nearby community garden. I walk, use public transportation, or carpool. And I reuse or recycle just about everything.

There are many people in this country who enjoy a life free from money worries. But not all. Poverty and desperation exist in America. And poverty is rampant in the rest of the world. Here at my home in Oregon, my motto is "I live simply, so others may simply live." My mother's words of wisdom still guide my choices today.

I believe my small efforts to protect the planet, save scarce resources for others, and enjoy what I am fortunate to have will make a difference. Small efforts on my part can make a big difference to someone else.

PATRICIA ANDERSON is a retired social worker, aging hippie, part-time writer, and knitting addict who moved from the Ozarks to the Pacific Northwest to be closer to her children and grandchildren. The author of a book of essays called *Down Home Musings*, Ms. Anderson lives in Wood Village, Oregon, with her two Labradors and one kitty.

Grace Is a Gift

∾

LAURA DURHAM

It doesn't always make sense to me, but when ambiguities such as grace and love manifest themselves, I'm moved by the clarity they bring.

The spring I was in the third grade, my teacher planned activities to celebrate the season. For weeks I looked forward to making treats and dying eggs. I remember telling my mom how much fun it was going to be, and I imagined what colors and designs I would choose. Before the big day, my teacher told us to come to class on Friday with a hollowed-out egg. We were also told to bring our spelling test signed by a parent, and if we didn't, the teacher warned, we would sit out from the activities.

At nine years old, I was the perfect student. I was studious, I was obedient, and I was responsible. So when I forgot to bring my spelling test that Friday, I was devastated. I knew what the consequence would be. When my class jumped from their chairs to collect art supplies, I sat still at my desk examining my perfect, hollowed-out egg, fighting the inevitable tears.

It wasn't long before my teacher pulled me aside. She knelt down and told me I should join the rest of the class. With tears in her eyes, she told me I could bring my spelling test on Monday. And then she gave me a hug.

I couldn't believe it. My disappointment disappeared with this unexpected gift.

Twenty years later, I still remember that moment. Even though I fell short of what was required of me, my teacher graced me with love and understanding. She could have stood her ground and let me sit out as an example to the other students, but she knew punishing me for this small mistake wouldn't teach me a new lesson. The lesson I learned that day was how much grace can lift someone's spirit.

Yet, I seem to have a hard time grasping grace in my life. I sometimes subscribe to the idea of karma: what goes around comes around. But then I remember that balancing a behavioral checkbook is detrimental to my happiness. If I'm constantly keeping count of what I feel I'm entitled to, I may never be satisfied. If I'm blessed beyond what I deserve, I might never feel worthy. I must remind myself that I know better. Not everyone is punished for breaking the rules, just as not everyone is rewarded for their efforts. Life may not be fair, but when I think about it, more often than not I'm on the fortunate side of the imbalance. And this moves me to offer the same grace to others.

I believe in being gracious to others, and I believe in accepting others' graciousness whether I've earned it or not. Sometimes you are blessed simply because someone loves you. And that is why grace is a gift—not a reward.

LAURA DURHAM lives in Salt Lake City, where she works for several arts organizations, including the Utah Arts Council, the Salt Lake Gallery Stroll, and *15 Bytes*, a visual arts e-zine. She also sings with the Utah Chamber Artists. Ms. Durham enjoys music, cooking, traveling, writing, and sharing stories with anyone who has the patience to listen to them.

The Sisterhood of Roller Derby

ERIN BLAKEMORE

When I first stepped onto the rink, I had no idea that by strapping on some pads and snapping a helmet into place I'd be taking a step toward changing my whole life. Now I know better.

They're secretaries and moms by day, but every woman who walks through the door of the Wagon Wheel roller rink has an alter ego. Sure, they masquerade behind funny names like Rockett and Ivona Killeau, but every skater in my roller derby league is an athlete in disguise, a rough-and-tumble, hard-core wonder woman who doesn't fear putting her body in danger on a daily basis.

At first I didn't think I would fit in. What does a bespectacled geek really have in common with a bunch of mean roller derby babes? To me, they were pinups on skates—sexy, powerful women with something to prove. That was before I started the grueling ritual of skating drills that taxed my body and my mind to the outer limits of endurance—and changed my insides to go along with my newly muscular frame.

Through months of training it became clear: I was unstable on my skates, but that wasn't my only problem. I was too inhibited, a buttoned-up woman on the verge of a quarter-life crisis. I had just moved to a new state, ready to start a new life. Joining the roller derby was just another move in a long chain of flustered and floundering attempts to redefine myself in terms of what I could be rather than what I did for a living.

And I found I wasn't alone. Through divorce, death, and bankruptcy, lost jobs and lost boyfriends, the women of the Denver Roller Dolls are there at the rink four times a week beating each other up—and building each other up. My roller persona, Audrey Rugburn, is no different—she doesn't take no for an answer. She's tough and selfish and undeniably strong. And before too long, her power started bleeding into my everyday life. I've gone from mistrusting my own instincts to knowing true confidence.

Some dismiss the roller derby as campy sports entertainment that's past its prime. Others think that just because I skate in fishnets it's not a real contact sport. But I laugh at these critics and others who have reared their ugly heads in the year since I've begun my transformation from doormat to derby queen. With the sisterhood and support of fifty other women, I know that whatever life flings my way will be skated over with pride and flair. After all, my alter ego is buff, brash, and rarin' to go—even when my insides quiver like a set of sore thighs.

Sometimes, life's scariest changes start with a bold external transformation. I've become one with Audrey Rugburn, a persona I trust, because she taught me to never doubt myself.

That's why I believe in roller derby.

After cofounding the Denver Roller Dolls, ERIN BLAKEMORE hung up her skates in 2007. She lives and works in Boulder, Colorado, where she cheers on her sister skaters as a rabid roller derby fan. Ms. Blakemore's debut book, *The Heroine's Bookshelf*, was published by Harper in 2010.

Caring Makes Us Human

TROY CHAPMAN

When the scruffy orange cat showed up in the prison yard, I was one of the first to go out there and pet it. I hadn't touched a cat or a dog in over twenty years. I spent at least twenty minutes crouched down by the Dumpster behind the kitchen as the cat rolled around and luxuriated beneath my attention. What he was expressing outwardly, I was feeling inwardly.

It was an amazing bit of grace to feel him under my hand and know that I was enriching the life of another creature with something as simple as my care. I believe that caring for something or someone in need is what makes us human.

Over the next few days I watched other prisoners responding to the cat. Every yard period, a group of prisoners gathered there. They stood around talking and taking turns petting the cat. These were guys you wouldn't usually find talking to each other. Several times I saw an officer in the group—not chasing people away, but just watching and seeming to enjoy it along with the prisoners.

Bowls of milk and water appeared, along with bread, wisely placed under the edge of the Dumpster to keep the seagulls from getting it. The cat was obviously a stray and in pretty bad shape. One prisoner brought out his small, blunt-tipped scissors and trimmed burrs and matted fur from its coat.

People said, "That cat came to the right place. He's getting treated like a king." This was true. But as I watched, I was also thinking about what the cat was doing for us.

There's a lot of talk about what's wrong with prisons in America. We need more programs; we need more psychologists or treatment of various kinds. Some even talk about making prisons more kind, but I think what we really need is a chance to practice kindness ourselves. Not receive it, but give it.

After more than two decades here, I know that kindness is not a value that's encouraged. It's often seen as a weakness. Instead, the culture encourages keeping your head down, minding your own business, and never letting yourself be vulnerable.

For a few days a raggedy cat disrupted this code of prison culture. They've taken him away now, hopefully to a decent home—but it did my heart good to see the effect he had on me and the men here. He didn't have a PhD, he wasn't a criminologist or a psychologist, but by simply saying, "I need some help here," he did something important for us. He needed us—and we need to be needed. I believe we all do.

TROY CHAPMAN is a writer, artist, and musician incarcerated at Kinross Correctional Facility in Kincheloe, Michigan. He has developed a system of wholeness ethics into a weekly program for fellow inmates and is the author of *Stepping Up: Wholeness Ethics for Prisoners (and Those Who Care about Them)*.

Satisfaction with a Job Well Done

NANCY PIETERS MAYFIELD

When I was in college twenty-five years ago, I spent four summers working in housekeeping at a luxury hotel in downtown Chicago. In other words, I was a maid. Each May, I traded my book bag and library card for a black uniform dress, a white apron, and a dust cloth.

I did not enter the world of housekeeping enthusiastically. My friends had summer jobs making ice cream sundaes, hawking accessories at the mall, or lifeguarding at the outdoor pool. I had been hoping to get a job as an office assistant for the county prosecutor: decent pay, an air-conditioned office, the gold standard for summer jobs.

When that fell through, the only option left was to join a handful of college students who took the twenty-five-minute train ride downtown each morning to work as maids during the busy summer convention season in Chicago.

It was tiring work, cleaning up to eighteen rooms a day. My poor attitude reflected my disdain for scrubbing toilets, changing bed linens, dusting, and vacuuming eight hours a day for the comfort of total strangers who rarely left a tip. I thought it was beneath me, a fledging journalist. My maid work was passable, my effort mediocre, until the day I was assigned to the eighteenth floor, which was a floor of newly renovated suites.

That was Lorena's regular floor. The only time another maid set foot on it was on Lorena's day off. If you left a trace of soap scum in the bathtub, a crumpled tissue under the bed, or a pillow unfluffed, Lorena would hunt you down when she returned, as I found out firsthand. She ended her lecture to me with, "Take some pride in your work."

She did. And so did Rosalie, Helen, Annette, Pearlie, Earline, and all of the other career maids with more than one hundred years of experience among them. Their commitment to doing a good job and their belief that their work was a reflection of their character stuck with me throughout my professional career. I learned a lot from them those four summers.

Not a week went by without one of them offering some firm but friendly advice: "Where's your commode brush? You don't have one? How do you expect to get that bowl clean?" or "You don't want to use that cleanser. That one will leave too much grit." Don't cut corners. Do the right thing.

Their pride in a job well done was reflected in how they carried themselves. They left the building at the end of the day in floral print dresses and carefully applied lipstick. They looked like they could have been attending an afternoon tea. And, most often, they were smiling and laughing, cheerfully bidding their coworkers a good evening.

Happy and content with a job well done. I believe there is respect in any job if you work hard and try your best.

NANCY PIETERS MAYFIELD is a writer who lives in Dixon, Illinois, with her husband, Trevis. A former newspaper reporter in northwest Indiana and a journalism teacher at Saint Mary-of-the-Woods College, Ms. Mayfield enjoys reading, writing, kayaking, and cooking. Her bathroom is always spotless.

The World Is Imperfect

SUZANNE CLEARY

I believe in imperfection.

I have worn glasses since the age of four. My first pair had pink cat's-eye frames with a thick foam patch covering the left lens so that my right eye, my "lazy eye," would grow strong. Whenever a classmate made fun of my glasses, I explained the lazy-eye phenomenon. I spoke with a calm self-assurance that I still occasionally hear in myself. And when I hear it, I smile and remember that child who did not see her body as imperfect, who did not see her classmate's teasing as other than pure curiosity.

Since kindergarten, I have learned to see imperfection. And I regularly relearn. Every time I pick up a magazine I learn how to maximize my investments, minimize my waistline, and organize my closets. Everywhere, perfection glares.

G. K. Chesterton wrote, "Anything worth doing is worth doing badly." I may not understand him perfectly, but I think he is saying, "Go ahead. Give it a shot." I believe in imperfection, because if I believed otherwise I would not dare to cook a meal, knit a sweater, stand up in front of a class, or write a poem. Imperfection invites me to step up to a challenge.

My art teacher says, "Hang up your bad drawings on the wall, not just your good ones. You learn more from your bad drawings than your good drawings." Creativity risks failure, perhaps *requires* failure. It thrives on exploration, discovery, play.

In childhood my favorite books were joke books. I trace my love of language to reading aloud from these with my father. Imperfection often is the key to jokes. Most humor arises from incongruity, the unexpected shift in which logic or perspective goes wrong.

Here is my favorite joke: Do you know why bagpipers always march while they play? They are trying to get away from the noise.

My great-aunt Margaret Cleary Bauer also believed in imperfection. During an annual physical her doctor broached a delicate topic: "You know," he said, "you probably would feel better if you lost five pounds." Aunt Margaret responded, "Doctor, I am ninety-four years old. How good do I have to feel?"

How good, indeed. That's the question. I can always feel better, look better, do better. I can learn more, sell more, buy more. I can do more, and do it faster. But what is the price of this perfection? Joy. I feel robbed of joy. The good, which is imperfect, becomes not good enough.

I believe in imperfection, ultimately, because I have to. The world is imperfect, and I choose to love the world. This is not easy. I believe in the bagpiper's labored song, in lopsided eyeglasses, in children who make fun of what they don't understand, because they teach me patience, discipline, compassion—qualities I possess only intermittently, imperfectly.

SUZANNE CLEARY is a poet whose most recent book is *Trick Pear*, published by Carnegie Mellon University Press in 2007. Her current eyeglasses have black plastic frames.

Peace Can Happen

CHRISTINE KINGERY

My grandmother was born in northern Russia to a large family of fourteen siblings. She was sixteen years old when World War II broke out. Her first job was going onto the battlefields to dismantle bombs that hadn't exploded.

She was captured by the Nazis when she was seventeen and taken to a "work camp" in Germany. They shaved off her waist-length hair and tortured her. Grandma never saw her parents and siblings again. Her mother died when Grandma was young. Her father was taken away to Siberia for political treason and never seen again, and most of her siblings died in the war.

My resourceful grandmother escaped the camp and worked for many months as a nurse in underground movements in Germany and Belgium. She was captured by the Nazis again and put into another concentration camp. This one was bigger. A death camp. There she met my grandfather, and the two escaped.

After the war, they had nowhere to go. They returned to a concentration camp in Stuttgart, which had been converted into a displacement camp. There my mother was born and raised. It took my grandparents eleven years to finally come to America.

When I was young, I heard many stories about the war. One day when I was eight, I said to my grandmother, "I hate the Germans for what they did to you! Don't you just get so *mad* at them?"

I'll never forget my grandmother's response. She said in her broken English, "The Germans are my friends. When I escaped and had nowhere to go, the Germans gave me food, shelter, and clothes. They were my friends even in the camps. The Germans are the kindest people I know."

Her answer shocked me, and it was my first introduction to the meaning of compassion.

A few years later, in high school, I had the chance to visit Japan. My host family took me to Nagasaki to the Atomic Bomb Museum and Peace Park. It was the fiftieth anniversary of the bombings. I was terrified, being *so* white skinned and *so* American!

I walked slowly through the crowded exhibits, looking at the black-and-white photographs. In every picture, in every Japanese victim's face, I saw my grandmother's reflection looking back at me. The experience was overwhelming, and I began to cry. I needed to get air, so I went outside.

There in Peace Park, beautiful, colorful origami cranes—thousands of them!—were draped over statues and trees. I sat on a bench and cried. I cried for the suffering of the Japanese people. I cried for the suffering of my own family in Europe during World War II. I cried for the suffering yet to be caused by wars sure to come.

An old Japanese lady saw me on the bench. She was about my grandmother's age, and she spoke very little English. She sat next to me and put her wrinkled hands in mine. She said, "Peace starts right here. Peace starts with you and me. It starts today."

She was right. I didn't have to suffer personally in order to understand the pain of others. I believe that through compassion, peace can happen. It echoes from the heart of a single individual.

CHRISTINE KINGERY is the director of marketing for an engineering firm in upstate New York. She enjoys working on public infrastructure projects because she believes parks, roads, and trails can positively enhance a community. In her free time, Ms. Kingery canoes with her cat and explores local history.

A Priceless Lesson in Humility

FELIPE MORALES

A few years ago, I took a sightseeing trip to Washington, D.C. I saw many of our nation's treasures, and I also saw a lot of our fellow citizens on the street—unfortunate ones, like panhandlers and homeless folks.

Standing outside the Ronald Reagan Center, I heard a voice say, "Can you help me?" When I turned around, I saw an elderly, blind woman with her hand extended. In a natural reflex, I reached into my pocket, pulled out all my loose change, and placed it on her hand without even looking at her. I was annoyed at being bothered by a beggar.

But the blind woman smiled and said, "I don't want your money. I just need help finding the post office."

In an instant, I realized what I had done. I acted with prejudice—I judged another person simply for what I assumed she had to be.

I hated what I saw in myself. This incident reawakened my core belief. It reaffirmed that I believe in humility, even though I'd lost it for a moment.

The thing I had forgotten about myself is that I am an immigrant. I left Honduras and arrived in the United States at the age of fifteen. I started my new life with two suitcases, my brother and sister, and a strong, no-nonsense mother. Through the years I have been a dishwasher, a roofer, a cashier, a mechanic, and a pizza delivery driver, among many other humble jobs, and eventually I became a network engineer.

In my own life, I have experienced many open acts of prejudice. I remember a time at age seventeen, I was a busboy and I heard a father tell his little boy that if he did not do well in school, he would end up like me. I have also witnessed the same kind of treatment toward family and friends, so I know what it's like, and I should have known better when I encountered the blind woman.

But now, living in my American middle-class lifestyle, it is too easy to forget my past, to forget who I am and where I have been, and to lose sight of where I want to be going. That blind woman on the streets of Washington, D.C., cured me of my self-induced blindness. She reminded me of my belief in humility and to always keep my eyes and heart open.

By the way, I helped that lady to the post office. And in writing this essay, I hope to thank her for the priceless lesson.

FELIPE MORALES was born in Tegucigalpa, Honduras, in 1974, and immigrated with his family to Tampa, Florida, in 1990. He now lives with his wife and children in Rowlett, Texas, where he enjoys spending time with his family and friends.

Finding Out What's Under
Second Base

LEX URBAN

My belief was formed eighteen years ago as a five-year-old kid during my first of many seasons of Little League baseball. My friend, Patrick, was on second base when I came up to bat. I sent a line drive out to left field, and after admiring my hit for a while (that momentary pause that drives coaches and parents nuts), I took off running in the direction of first base. Patrick, however, had yet to start running. In fact, he hadn't even left second base. Instead of running for third, Patrick had picked up the base to explore what was underneath. Apparently the mystery that had plagued kids for centuries—what could possibly be hiding underneath second base?—needed to be solved immediately. The fact that it was the second inning of our first T-ball game was of no consequence.

What followed were howls of laughter from many kids and even a few adults. I don't remember if we won the game, if I made it to second base, or if Patrick took the base with him as he advanced to third. What I do remember, and what has become a core philosophy of mine, is that I should always take the time to find out what's underneath second base.

Looking underneath second base is about living for the moment. It's not caring if others think what I'm doing is stupid or foolish. It is about being honest with myself and doing what makes me happy and not bowing to outside pressures. It is a reminder that I should look beneath the surface of things, and more important, people. Everyone has a story—a series of significant and insignificant experiences that precede each moment of their lives. I am more patient and understanding, because I realize that the story may be a painful and stressful one.

After college graduation I did not get a high-paying job on Wall Street like many of my classmates did. I decided to dedicate a year to full-time community service as an AmeriCorps volunteer at City Year in Washington, D.C. I tutored kids of all ages in math and reading. I saw firsthand the impact of painful and stressful experiences. A hardened exterior usually hid a much softer individual on the inside. A kid who told me off on the first day later expressed sadness that he didn't get to see me over the Thanksgiving break. I saw the power of giving my time to help others. It has truly been the most memorable experience of my life thus far.

No longer a five-year-old without a care in the world, I have been introduced to the adult concepts of planning, responsibility, and maturity. No one can deny the importance of the future, but no one can guarantee its presence, either. I try not to get so wrapped up in planning for the future that I forget to enjoy what's right in front of me. Taking time to look underneath second base reminds me that it's the journey and not the destination that counts.

Looking under second base reminds me to take the time to appreciate things. It reminds me that the daily grind and the hustle and bustle of a fast-paced world is a voluntary activity. I can choose how I live my life. I choose to always take the time to find out what's under second base.

LEX URBAN is the former captain of the two-time National Champion Williams College Men's Tennis team. Mr. Urban served a year as an AmeriCorps member of City Year in Washington, D.C., where he now lives and practices law.

Accomplishing Big Things in Small Pieces

WILLIAM WISSEMANN

I carry a Rubik's Cube in my backpack. Solving it quickly is a terrific conversation starter, and it is surprisingly impressive to girls. I've been asked to solve the cube on the New York City subway, at a track meet in Westchester, and at a café in Paris. I usually ask people to try it first. They turn the cube over in their hands, halfheartedly make a few moves, and then sheepishly hand it back. They don't even know where to begin. That's exactly what it was like for me to learn how to read. Letters and words were scrambled and out of sequence. Nothing made sense, because I'm dyslexic.

Solving the Rubik's Cube has made me believe that sometimes you have to take a few steps back to move forward. This was a mirror of my own life when I had to leave public school after the fourth grade. It's embarrassing to admit, but I still couldn't consistently spell my full name correctly.

As a fifth-grader at a new school, specializing in what's called language processing disorder, I had to start over. Memorizing symbols for letters, I learned the pieces of the puzzle of language, the phonemes that make up words. I spent the next four years learning how to learn and finding strategies that allowed me to return to my district's high school with the ability to communicate my ideas and express my intelligence.

It took me four weeks to teach myself to solve the cube—the same amount of time it took the inventor, Erno Rubik. Now, I can easily solve the $3 \times 3 \times 3$, the $4 \times 4 \times 4$, and the Professor's Cube, the $5 \times 5 \times 5$. I discovered that just before a problem is solved it can look like a mess, and then suddenly you can find the solution. I believe that progress comes in unexpected leaps.

Early in my Rubik's career, I became so frustrated that I took the cube apart and rebuilt it. I believe that sometimes you have to look deeper and in unexpected places to find answers. I noticed that I can talk or focus on other things and still solve the cube. There must be an independent part of my brain at work, able to process information.

The Rubik's Cube taught me that to accomplish something big, it helps to break the problem down into small pieces. I learned that it's important to spend a lot of time thinking, to try to find connections and patterns. I believe that there are surprises around the corner. And, that the cube and I are more than the sum of our parts.

Like a difficult text or sometimes like life itself, the Rubik's Cube can be a frustrating puzzle. So I carry a cube in my backpack as a reminder that I can attain my goals, no matter what obstacles I face.

And did I mention that being able to solve the cube is surprisingly impressive to girls?

WILLIAM TYLER WISSEMANN was raised in Hastings-on-Hudson, New York. He will graduate from Bard College with dual Bachelor of Arts degrees in computer science and photography in May 2012. Mr. Wissemann was honored to be asked to present his essay and demonstrate the Rubik's Cube at College Night at the Walters Art Museum in 2009.

I Have to See the World

VEENA MUTHURAMAN

Saint Augustine once said, "The world is a book and those who do not travel read only a page." Me, I want to read the entire library.

I believe in going places. I believe in getting out of my apartment and into my car or a plane and going to see a totally new place. I want to see the world in all its glory, with my own eyes and in the flesh; television and Google Earth just won't do. I believe that travel opens one's mind to new cultures and perspectives; it affords one a broader vision of life, a vision that does not come by sitting within the four walls of one's home.

I grew up in a small city in southern India. I was all of seven years old when we went to visit my grandparents for my monthlong summer vacation. Until then, my world consisted of our small apartment and our bustling city surrounded by pristine beaches, coconut groves, and misty mountains. I was aware of the existence of a different world beyond home, but surely I didn't want to spend my vacation in some backward village in a rural district of an alien state. We boarded a state transport bus, and I sat by the window, sulking.

Soon I noticed the wetlands giving away to parched land. The cities we were passing now were more crowded than the ones we left behind; people were darker, like me, and they were dressed differently. When I finally got to my grandparents' village, the landscape and the people were so vastly different from what I was used to that I was over-whelmed. A village with just one street, houses with tiled roofs, and all of the houses had barns with cows and bulls inside! I wanted to go see them, but I was scared. All of the village kids looked at me as if I was an alien from outer space, and I promptly hid behind my mother's sari and refused to talk to anyone.

Over the next couple of weeks, I slowly got to know the place and the people; I learned the other kids' games and played with their toys. They taught me how to milk a cow, how to catch fish in the nearby stream, and how to steal mangoes from my grandpa's grove. And finally, when it was time to go back home, I was sad to leave but ready for new adventures. Because by then I seemed to have realized that our little corner of the universe and the people who live here are too diverse and too wonderful to be left unseen. I had to see the world.

Years later, on a plane to this country I now call home, it was this desire to travel, this conviction that there's so much to see and to cherish on this earth than just the familiar places of my childhood, that kept me from breaking down and staying in India. My intense longing for my family, my friends, and the places I loved was countered by my anticipation for what I would find in the New World. And America has not disappointed me. The sloping Alleghenies of Pennsylvania where I spent my school years, the tall skyscrapers of Chicago where I live now, the colors of a New England fall, the deep crevices of the Grand Canyon all reinforce my essential belief that only by leaving the security of your home will you find the beauty of the world around you.

Mark Twain said, "Travel is fatal to prejudice, bigotry, and narrow-mindedness. . . . Broad, wholesome, charitable views of men and things cannot be acquired by vegetating in one little corner of the earth all one's lifetime."

I couldn't agree more.

When she is not traveling, VEENA MUTHURAMAN can be found deeply submerged in Excel worksheets while simultaneously dreaming of new travel adventures. Ecuador is next on her list, but Ms. Muthuraman will need to outsource care of her eleven-month-old before she can go. She currently lives in London, England.

Deciding to Live

∽

KIJ JOHNSON

I believe I am a climber.

Three years ago, a series of medical and personal crises took what was a clinical depression and made it something much darker.

I thought of it as falling—as jumping—off a bridge on a rainy, winter day: three seconds in the air before I hit the water and plunged deep into the icy cold, my heavy coat pulling me deeper. And the surface far overhead—too far away.

This is the question that kept me from making the image a real one: What if I changed my mind? After jumping into the water, the air in my lungs would fail me before I could swim back to the living world. I would know for those last seconds that I did want to live after all, but it would be too late.

I'm not sure why I started climbing. I walked through the door of the local climbing gym one day on a whim. It was an alien world: strong, beautiful men and women, towering walls under sodium vapor lights, white dust filling the air. Light instead of dark. Up instead of down. It was in every way the opposite of what was inside me.

The second time I climbed, I got to a move in which I was sure I would fall. I was twenty-five feet up on a rope, but I didn't know yet that I could trust it. I heard my voice say out loud, "I have a choice here: fear or joy." What I meant was climb or don't climb, live or die.

In the more than two years since then, I have climbed hundreds of days—inside and out, sometimes tied to a rope, often not.

I do pay a price here. My body can be so bruised from hitting walls that people ask me about my home situation. Nine months ago, I broke my leg and ankle. I healed fast, but the risk remains. Next time I might not.

Climbing requires a cold-blooded decision to live. If I am inattentive or careless, I will fall. Every time I climb at the gym or rope up for a route outside or go bouldering—which is climbing without a rope, and it is often more dangerous—I am taking a risk. And I am committing to staying alive.

Now, I believe in climbing, in not jumping. Jumping would have been easy—just step over the bridge railing and let go. Climbing is harder but worth it. I believe that deciding to live was the right decision.

There's no way to describe the terrible darkness of depression in a way that nondepressed people can understand. Now, I'm less focused on the darkness. Instead, I think about the joy I feel in conquering it and the tool I used.

I am a climber, and I am alive.

KIJ JOHNSON is a writer whose fiction has won the Nebula Award and the World Fantasy Award, and she has been nominated for the Hugo Award. She lives in North Carolina and climbs wherever and whenever she can. Ms. Johnson is at work on a series of essays about climbing.

Walking in the Light

PAUL THORN

I don't want to be a God-fearing man. I believe in religion without fear.

I grew up in a Pentecostal-type faith in northeast Mississippi called the Church of God of Prophecy, where my father was the pastor. At the age of twelve, I was sent to a summer Bible camp where fear was the motivation for belief. One night the counselors staged a Russian takeover of the camp, simulating the assassination of our camp director. Real shotgun blasts scared us all to our knees, and we begged God for salvation.

At the age of seventeen, I was disfellowshipped from my church for having premarital sex with my girlfriend. Since my father was the pastor, a meeting was arranged with me, my dad, and my Sunday school teacher. I was given two options: stand and confess my sins in front of the congregation and be forgiven or continue my evil ways and no longer be in the club. I chose to be disfellowshipped and became officially unaffiliated with the church.

I moved out of the parsonage, got a job in a furniture factory, and bought a used mobile home for $6,000. People from the church would come by my trailer from time to time to tell me they were still praying for me and that they hoped I would come back to Jesus before I wound up in hell. I just stared at the ground the way you would with a schoolyard bully and hoped they'd go away.

As the years passed by, opportunity took me all over the United States and to other countries as well. I saw churches everywhere I went, and I noticed something I'd never seen before. I met people who didn't pray to Jesus. You have to understand, where I come from the people who tried to teach me about God by using fear also kept me from learning about other paths to God. Any variation was described as a trick of the devil.

But I saw good, sincere Muslims, Buddhists, and Jews all walking in the light—as they knew it. I started to believe that no one is capable of knowing God's specific identity, so I decided to seek him down my own path, because I believe that's what he wants me to do. I talk to him daily.

He never says anything back, but I know he's listening. I thank him for my family and friends, and I thank him for the good life I have. I still have problems like anyone else, but overall there's peace in my heart.

The people who were trying to get me to God used fear and intimidation like a hammer, beating into submission anyone who dared to question their brand of absolute truth.

The higher power I now pray to gives me love, joy, and comfort. And I'm not afraid of him. I had to break away from the God I was supposed to believe in to find the God I could believe in.

Singer-songwriter PAUL THORN was born in Wisconsin and raised in Tupelo, Mississippi. He was a professional boxer and worked in a furniture factory before being discovered playing guitar at a local pizzeria. Mr. Thorn's latest album is *Pimps and Preachers*.

The Perfect Merge

LORI VERMEULEN

I believe that the strength of a person's faith is inversely proportional to the distance she travels before merging when entering a construction zone.

"Merge!" the blinking yellow lights shout. "Merge! Go left! Move over immediately!" What's a body to do when faced with such clear direction as this? If I merge immediately, I will be obeying the law. Furthermore, I will be safely in the correct lane when only one lane remains. What else can I do but merge?

Well, there is, of course, a second option. The alternative is to selfishly speed ahead while leaving those early mergers in my dust. I can pass everybody and sneak into the merge lane at the last possible moment. This choice would put me in first place, and isn't first place the best place to be?

This is a simple choice if I am thinking only of myself. The decision only becomes complicated when I consider both the actions and the welfare of my fellow mergers. If all drivers merge as soon as possible, everyone will be in the right place when the two lanes become one. No one will be left behind. A perfect merge means that no one is delayed for even one second. But, let's face it: if just one individual chooses to speed ahead, a delay will occur for everyone when the entire merged lane must stop to let the speedy one in. And, in that case, he who merged first will wait the longest. Do I want to be the offender? The one who just "can't wait" and ultimately destroys the synchronous beauty of the perfect merge?

To love one's enemies is to merge early and wave to the guy who speeds on. Isn't that what all the great religions teach? I am a human being, and therefore I have a choice. I can choose to be selfish and a step ahead of everyone else, or I can choose to be generous and accept the risk of being left behind.

It is an act of faith to merge early. My faith in making this choice is not in the belief that all will merge early and no one will be delayed. Oh, no. As long as there are human beings, there will be those who will fail and fall short, and there will be times when I will be one of the fallen ones. My faith is in the belief that sacrifice for others is inherently good and making the choice to do good is the gift of being human.

I'm now a college administrator and professor, as well as a parent, so I've had numerous opportunities to look at many different perceptions of fairness and try to understand them. I tell my students and my own children that the important thing is that everybody has a choice, but the only choices you can control are your own. We find unfairness everywhere in life. I believe it's best to accept this and choose to do the right thing.

So I merge early because I can. And I hope that I smile and wave when stopping to let my fellow man in ahead of me.

LORI VERMEULEN is the dean of the College of Arts and Sciences and a professor of chemistry at West Chester University of Pennsylvania. She has been married to her high school sweetheart for twenty-nine years and is the mother of three beautiful children.

Listening Is Powerful Medicine

∼👂

ALICIA M. CONILL, M.D.

I believe listening is powerful medicine.

Studies have shown it takes a physician about eighteen seconds to interrupt a patient after he or she begins talking.

It was Sunday. I had one last patient to see. I approached her room in a hurry and stood at the doorway. She was an older woman, sitting at the edge of the bed, struggling to put socks on her swollen feet. I crossed the threshold, spoke quickly to the nurse, and scanned her chart, noting that she was in stable condition. I was almost in the clear.

I leaned on the bed rail and looked down at her. She asked if I could help put on her socks. Instead, I launched into a monologue that went something like this: "How are you feeling? Your sugars and blood pressure were high but they're better today. The nurse mentioned you're anxious to see your son who's visiting you today. It's nice to have family visit from far away. I bet you really look forward to seeing him."

She stopped me with a stern, authoritative voice. "Sit down, doctor. This is my story, not your story."

I was surprised and embarrassed. I sat down. I helped her with the socks. She began to tell me that her only son lived around the corner from her, but she had not seen him in five years. She believed that the stress of this contributed greatly to her health problems. After hearing her story and putting on her socks, I asked if there was anything else I could do for her. She shook her head no and smiled. All she wanted me to do was to listen.

Each story is different. Some are detailed; others are vague. Some have a beginning, middle, and end. Others wander without a clear conclusion. Some are true, others not. Yet all of those things do not really matter. What matters to the storyteller is that the story is heard—without interruption, assumption, or judgment.

Listening to someone's story costs less than expensive diagnostic testing but is key to healing and diagnosis.

I have often thought of what that woman taught me and reminded myself of the importance of stopping, sitting down, and truly listening. And, not long after, in an unexpected twist, I became the patient, with a diagnosis of multiple sclerosis at age thirty-one. Now, twenty years later, I sit all the time—in a wheelchair.

For as long as I could, I continued to see patients from my chair but had to resign when my hands were affected. I still teach medical students and other health care professionals, but now from the perspective of both physician *and* patient.

I tell them I believe in the power of listening. I tell them I know firsthand that immeasurable healing takes place within me when someone stops, sits down, and listens to my story.

ALICIA CONILL, M.D., is a clinical associate professor at the University of Pennsylvania School of Medicine. A native of Cuba, Dr. Conill also directs the nonprofit Conill Institute, which provides education to increase empathy, knowledge, and awareness about people living with chronic illness and physical disability.

Semper Fidelis

ANDREW PARADIS

My foundational belief, the one thing I find that I can count on in myself, and that I cling to in times of crisis, was formed during my service in the U.S. Marines. Their motto is "Semper Fidelis," which means "always faithful."

In the Corps, that motto translated to the idea that you never leave your partner, especially in times of great need. You are there not to save or protect yourself, but to make sure your buddies are safe and protected; simply put, the mission and your comrades are more important than you are, and you realize quickly that you are engaged in events far larger than yourself.

Since serving in the Corps, I have been challenged to remain always faithful. Several years ago, my wife, who has a physical disability (Ehlers-Danlos syndrome), began suffering from an undiagnosed mental illness, bipolar disorder. In the months leading up to her eventual diagnosis and treatment, she attempted suicide three times. I did all I could to keep up as much of a normal life as possible, especially for our young daughter, who also has Ehlers-Danlos. I didn't want her to think of her mom as crazy, as a person who couldn't be her mom anymore.

Over the winter my endurance began to wear thin; I felt alone in an emotional storm, all guidance systems offline. There were times of deep weakness in which I almost gave in to my wife's late-night whispered pleadings to help her kill herself: "Just turn the other way," "Just take Ana to visit your parents for the weekend." But in the few islands of calm, I was able to somehow rekindle the spirit of that Marine Corps motto. I decided that if nothing else, I would not quit on the woman I loved; I would not quit on our daughter. If it brought me to my knees, so be it. I would see her through her recovery process. I needed to be there to make sure she was safe and protected, regardless of any impact that would have on me.

Now, four years later, my wife is on good meds and in good therapy, and she has regained her true, loving self. Our daughter has her mom back, I have my wife back, and she has herself back. And it is because of this fundamental belief, this notion that you never quit on those you love.

Semper Fi.

ANDREW PARADIS is a former U.S. Marine and current theoretical physicist/software engineer. He grew up in Fort Kent, Maine, with four younger brothers, who correctly tortured him for his many idiosyncrasies. He lives and works in western Maine with his wife and daughter and their dogs, cats, and horses.

Our Vulnerability Is
Our Strength

COLIN BATES

Most of my friends have recently graduated from college. Every so often one will call me up to grumble about their new job, telling me how underappreciated they feel or how they're not achieving the success they wanted. I enjoy listening to them. I think that's what friends are for. But it also gives me perspective on my own work.

I work with two developmentally disabled men, my bosses essentially, who each have profound mental retardation. They're loud without being able to speak. They're violent without understanding the consequences. They can't bathe themselves. They can't cook or work a job. Their behaviors range from catatonic to aggressive.

As a resident service assistant, I go to where these men live and help them in everything they do—bathing, dressing, cooking, feeding, cleaning, going to the bathroom—from the moment they wake until they go to bed. It pays nine bucks an hour.

Underappreciated? Try having your hair ripped out while changing a diaper. Try having the meal you've prepared thrown at you. Try being spit on.

The funny thing is, I love my job. I do. I know I'm young and still have a lot to learn, but here it is: I believe in helplessness, which is to say I believe we need other humans.

It isn't enough to be what our society has dubbed as successful. What we really need are others around us engaging, nurturing, listening, and willing to sacrifice their time and agendas. I don't care if you're the CEO of a multibillion-dollar company or a single mother with five kids. Nobody is completely self-sufficient, and so, in that way, we are all helpless. We're helpless unto each other.

The cool thing about the guys I work for is that they make their needs explicit. Things that take seconds for most of us, like changing socks, can take hours for them, but their vulnerability isn't a handicap so much as an example. Being with them, encouraging them—"Yes, the socks are on! The socks are off!"—puts things into perspective.

Most of the people I know are embarrassed by what they can't do. They see it as a sign of weakness and consequently walk around with burdened hearts. For my generation the notion that success equals fulfillment has been pounded into our brains as if it were the truth. My generation is being told that if you can't do something alone, if you're not smart enough or capable enough, then you've failed.

So far, the turning points in my life have not been the times I succeeded at something, but the times I've whispered, "I'm lost," or "Help me," or "I need a friend." In becoming helpless, I've allowed myself to be shaped and supported by those who love me—which makes helplessness a gift.

And I have my bosses to thank for it. We've discovered the joy of helping and being helped. I believe that sometimes our vulnerability is our strength.

COLIN BATES is a resident service assistant for people with mental disabilities and a student at Pennsylvania State University. He's finishing a degree in English and will pursue an MFA in creative writing. He lives in Bellefonte, Pennsylvania, with his cat, Cleo.

Patriotic Ponderings

JOAN SKIBA

As an army brat growing up in a military home, raised by military minds, I was receptive to all of the patriotic messages surrounding me. At a very early age, I recall memorizing a poem that always created a tremendous sense of pride as well as a healthy dose of goose bumps. A snippet of the poem is imprinted in my memory: "loyal hearts are beating high: / Hats off! / The flag is passing by!"

There was no question. I was the embodiment of a patriot, albeit a very young one. I was proud to be an American and knew in my young heart that the families in the military were very special and especially patriotic. Then I grew up.

I went to Ohio State in the sixties and saw firsthand the antiwar groups that frequented my college campus and dared to question my country's values and actions in Vietnam. Their messages alarmed me. I was putting all of my energy into my nursing education and had no inclination to question my government or the war. I felt hostility toward these dissenters and had no desire to hear any of their ideas. My naive, uninformed self believed that anyone opposing my government should just leave the country.

After graduation, I joined the Army Nurse Corps. I went to Vietnam and worked in an emergency room, tending to the casualties of the war. Within the first week I began to question my youthful paradigms. I looked into the eyes of a dying nineteen-year-old American and could not justify his death. I took care of a Vietcong soldier, tending to his wounds, knowing he would survive those wounds but ultimately lose his life to his captors. I cried as I plucked out pieces of small metal fragments from his body.

I gradually began to understand that war is patriotism on opposing sides. The uniforms differentiate the dogma but don't separate the grief. The uniforms define the combatants, but their losses are universal. The young American and Vietcong were patriots. Each loved, each defended, and each died for his country.

This is when I came to believe that a patriotic person can question and disagree with the country she loves.

I embrace my sense of belonging to this country, my love of this country, and the democratic values of this country. I staunchly endorse the patriotic right to question my country's values and its actions. As an American, I can question. As an American, I have the right to oppose any of my government's actions.

I believe it is my responsibility as a patriotic person to be informed and to never stop questioning.

And, yes, I still get goose bumps when watching our flag pass by.

After more than twenty years in emergency medicine, JOAN SKIBA returned to school to become an elementary school teacher. Her goal every year is to impress upon her young students the importance of critical thinking and the value of knowing, not simply believing. Ms. Skiba says war taught her that.

Opening the Door of Mercy

KARIN ROUND

One afternoon a couple of summers ago, just as the sky was darkening, a woman I didn't know stood sagging on our threshold, holding the screen door open. I saw the silhouette of her head through the window.

No, she answered me, she was not all right. She didn't feel well at all. So, I wondered, what was I supposed to do now?

This moment of decision had happened to me before. For almost nineteen years, we've lived here at the foot of a highway exit ramp. Our address is blandly suburban, but the highway often leads exhausted cars onto our curb.

Lately cell phones have diminished the flow, but we've met many people in distress. More diverse than our own community, these travelers have all asked for little things, such as the phone, a glass of water, or simply directions. All have been strangers to me.

Ours is a cynical, suspicious time. Conventional wisdom advises that to act as a good Samaritan is to be naive and risk terrible consequences. The news is full of stories about victims who unwittingly endanger themselves. I've no doubt that those are true stories, but the lesson rubs me the wrong way. Sometimes to do the right thing, you must take a risk. Must we fear all of those whom we don't know? If so, then how do we act or identify ourselves as neighbors or citizens when we won't greet one another without proper introductions and background checks? Is our own personal safety always the important consideration?

Our location forces me to make difficult choices. This is not some classroom debate for me. The highway makes it impossible to ignore the world and our relationship to it. When someone approaches us for help, I have to decide: Do I help them or not?

I wonder if people realize how final a step, how isolating, how evil it feels to literally shut the door on someone in need. I have done it. Sometimes I have been hostile to people, and although I can justify my actions, those are the moments I most regret.

I believe repeatedly rejecting others who need help endangers me, too. I'd rather risk my physical safety than my peace of mind. I'd rather live my life acting out of mercy than save it by living in fear and hostility.

So here where we live on that afternoon one summer when the woman was sinking like the sun on my front porch, I made my choice.

I opened the door.

KARIN ROUND is office manager for her family's hardware store in Massachusetts. She has studied nonfiction writing in a post-graduate program at Goucher College. Ms. Round continues to help travelers stranded on her doorstep.

The True Value of Life

SUDIE BOND NOLAND

I believe in the power of forgiveness and compassion. This act is so hard for many, including myself, but it is important to show an understanding heart when someone is faced with discord. It gives a chance, for some, to repent for their previous mistakes. I have come to learn the true nature of forgiveness over the years, beginning with a personal experience of mine that was life changing. It happened when I was thirteen.

I was riding with my friend's family in their car down a two-lane highway, when we were hit head-on by a drunk driver going sixty-five miles per hour. Eddy Jo was his name, and he was so intoxicated that one more beer would have killed him. Thankfully, everyone survived, although I came away from the accident with chronic back and neck pain, migraine headaches, and part of my kidney missing. It has nearly been a decade, and I am still in pain every day. Pain forever is a lot to swallow when you're young.

In court, the judge sentenced Eddy to twenty-five years in prison to make an example of the situation. I didn't understand the full extent of this when I was thirteen. I was upset about how the ignorance and actions of this person had changed my life forever.

As time went by, I began to think of Eddy in jail, away from his family, and how he must feel. I received letters from him, stating his remorse for his actions, and yet I couldn't bring myself to write back. I was so overwhelmed with so many different emotions that I didn't know what to say.

This is something I have been thinking about for a long time—something that I haven't looked at with a magnifying glass until this essay, actually.

I have now forgiven Eddy in my heart for his actions. I know that when he got into his car that night, he was too inebriated to even realize he was driving. He had a problem that got out of hand and out of his control.

I know Eddy didn't hit us as a malicious act in any way. It was a mistake, an awful mistake, but a mistake nonetheless.

I have the courage now to write to him. He will finally know how I feel when I send him this essay.

Forgiveness and compassion can be amazing feelings when you let them into your heart. People deserve a second chance to do the right thing, especially when one may have been caught up in circumstance. I don't think Eddy deserved twenty-five years in prison for his actions.

I am forever changed by him, but in some ways it has shown me the true value of life. Even though I struggle every day, I think it has made me a stronger person, a more loving and compassionate person.

For that, Eddy, I thank you.

SUDIE BOND NOLAND's experience in writing this essay has since propelled her on a personal healing journey and has awakened her own calling as a healer. Raised in Sarasota, Florida, she currently lives in Portland, Oregon. Ms. Noland is about to start her own practice as a Reiki Master and begin her schooling for a master's degree in Chinese medicine.

An Invitation to Dialogue

MADHUKAR RAO

I believe in the power of simple questions.

Back in 1974, when I was sixteen, my family moved from Massachusetts to New Jersey when my father changed jobs. It was a difficult transition for me: I was a junior in high school and had to leave the friends and community I'd known well to get used to new surroundings and attend a school where I was a stranger.

I remember how lonely I felt that first day of school. I was among the first students in the cafeteria at lunchtime, and I sat at a table in one corner of the large room. As more people filtered in, I noticed that all of the students sitting near me were black, and all of the white students were sitting on the other side of the room. I found this very strange—as if an invisible dividing line stretched across the cafeteria. This voluntary segregation was new to me, but I stayed where I was.

Some of the black students gave me odd looks as I sat alone, quietly eating my lunch. Partway through the lunch period, a tall, muscular, black student, whom I'll call Jake, walked over and stood across from me. He put his hands on the table and leaned forward. With his face close to mine, he firmly said, "Aren't you sitting with the wrong kind of people?"

Immediately, my fight-or-flight response kicked into high gear. What should I do? Should I defend myself? Should I let him intimidate me and undermine my self-respect? The other students suddenly became quiet, waiting for my response.

Jake had laid down the gauntlet, but I decided not to take the bait. I looked at him and innocently asked, "What do you mean, the wrong kind of people?"

He was dumbfounded. He stared at me for a few seconds, shook his head, and then walked away. My simple question had disarmed him. I had neither compromised my beliefs nor validated his racism. I slowly calmed down and ate the rest of my lunch without incident.

This experience taught me that simple questions like "What do you mean?" hold tremendous power. They signal a desire to understand and a willingness to listen. My simple question met intolerance with tolerance. I could have argued my right to remain where I sat or told Jake to leave me alone. But becoming defensive probably would have led to a lot of shouting—and I would have been lucky if it had ended there. Instead, I had invited him into a dialogue.

I like to think my question challenged Jake to confront his racism, but I'll never know for sure. I do know that when I saw him in the cafeteria the rest of that year, he looked at me and nodded as he passed. Although he never smiled at me, I took his acknowledgments as a sign that we had made a small connection.

I believe in the power of simple questions. Simple questions signal humility and an openness to listen non-judgmentally. They also serve as powerful weapons against intolerance.

A native of India, MADHUKAR RAO came to the United States with his parents at the age of three. He earned a bachelor's degree in chemical engineering from the New Jersey Institute of Technology and a PhD in materials science from Pennsylvania State University. He currently serves as chairman of the board of the Volunteers of America of Pennsylvania, a nonprofit social service organization. In his spare time, Mr. Rao enjoys reading, traveling, and practicing yoga.

Homeless but Not Hopeless:
A Man Finds His Soul

LES GAPAY

I was homeless for six-and-a-half years. But I believe not being hopeless got me out of it.

When a recession caused my writing and public relations business to tank in 2002, I gave up my apartment in Palm Springs, California, and started living at campgrounds in the back of my 1998 Toyota pickup.

I usually stayed in the southern California desert. But every summer, when it got too hot, I drove to camp in Montana, where I once lived.

At first I was still making a little money, so I camped at developed campgrounds with flush toilets, tables, and fire rings. But after a few years I was subsisting mostly on Social Security retirement and couldn't afford such luxuries. So I stayed at primitive campgrounds with outhouses, or once in a while at a Walmart parking lot. I ate at campgrounds or fast-food joints. I got on lists for subsidized senior housing.

In winter, the desert temperatures dropped as low as thirty degrees at night, and I snuggled up inside my sleeping bag on top of an air mattress. Sometimes I had to pile blankets atop my sleeping bag and sleep in several layers of clothes. When it rained, I covered my leaky camper shell with a tarp.

In the back of my truck at night I meditated on the Lord's Prayer. On Sundays, I went to church. I prayed for my family members, including my three brothers and two adult daughters, whom I never heard from. At first I prayed for work and a home, but eventually I accepted my situation, and it caused my stress to disappear.

Like Jacob in the Bible, I once asked God to come down and fight me like a man. But it did no good to argue with God, as Job also learned in the Bible. But even getting angry with God, I found, was a form of prayer.

I was better off than many homeless people. I had my truck and some Social Security income. I became eligible for Medicare, and that was a blessing with medical bills. My life wasn't so difficult if I didn't dwell on it.

My faith, once minimal, deepened as grappling with the difficulties and the evils of life turned me more to God. I knew where I was going in the long run, and it wasn't just to a campground.

In December 2008, I finally got to the top of a waiting list for an apartment in a complex for low-income seniors. Two charities helped me with the security deposit and the first month's rent. I retrieved my possessions from a storage unit, and opening my boxes was like an archeological dig into my past life: a TV, a stereo, suits and ties, photos of my daughters in happier days, a computer that was now obsolete.

After years of being homeless, I finally had a bed to sleep in and my own bathroom and kitchen. I could even use a heated pool to soothe my aching muscles. Every day in those first few weeks seemed like a gift.

The whole experience was a life lesson in the power of hope and faith, something that sustains me even today.

LES GAPAY, a freelance writer in Rancho Mirage, California, was a staff reporter for the *Wall Street Journal* and other newspapers and a public relations consultant for Fortune 500 companies. He is working on a book of spiritual-inspirational essays and another about his life.

The Power of Sleep

ANNE HOPPUS

I believe in the power of sleep. Pure, deep, easy sleep. Quiet, dark sleep, that removes you completely from the world. A good night's sleep.

Most mornings I drag myself out of bed, neither rested nor refreshed, starting the day already behind. I push my cat away, snap at my husband, and drive to work in a mildly angry daze. I'm not particularly a morning person, but it's not that. It's that most nights I stay up too late, stalked and driven by the to-do list that forever hovers before me. My eyes start to droop; my thoughts begin to wander. My body and the better parts of my brain signal me in every way possible that it is time to go to bed. But a nagging voice speaks up, pushes me ever onward, telling me that I have dishes and paperwork to do and miles to go before I sleep. And so I seldom go to bed when I should. I stay up too late, and my mornings (and my husband) suffer.

Oh, but those mornings when I have had enough sleep! Those mornings following nights in which I have successfully turned off my brain? Those mornings are gifts. I wake before the alarm and lie in bed, at peace with the light making its way through my window. My cat nuzzles against me, and I am happy to return her affection. I look at my husband, and my heart aches for a moment with love for him. I drive to work, waving other drivers ahead of me in traffic, preferring to have a couple more seconds of time out in the beautiful world.

On these days I am happier. I feel more love, more joy, more peace. I am better at my job. I think more clearly. I am a better wife, a better mother, a better pet owner. And, I get more done! On these days, the eternal to-do list is less daunting, more of a challenge than a judgment. With my newfound energy, I can clean house or wash clothes, I can write, I can grocery shop. Even better, on these days my well-rested mind and I can tell the to-do list to go to hell. We are smart enough to know that sometimes the best move is to lie completely still and just be. These are the days I live for.

I don't know how or when we stopped believing in sleep, when we relegated it to a status somewhere between "complete waste of time" and "something to do when dead," but it's time to take back our nights. We need our sleep. The world would be a better place if we were all less cranky, less irritable, less exhausted. Even if the dishes aren't done.

I believe in the power of sleep. It's right at the top of my to-do list.

ANNE HOPPUS is a working and writing mother of two girls. She lives in San Diego, California.

Where Wildflowers Grow

⸰

MAUREEN CRANE WARTSKI

Rain, the pelting, driving, summer rain that falls on these Carolinas, forced us to take shelter under the overhang of a store. After the wringing and shaking out and the first relief of being out of the downpour came the question: Now what?

"Maybe they sell umbrellas in the store," my husband said. He disappeared into the building and returned with a discovery. In the back of the store was a country-western nightclub. The band would be on in five minutes. Was I game?

It sure beat standing under the dripping eaves! We went inside and were seated, and in a few minutes the band began to play.

This was quite a band. The lead guitarist, blond and long-haired, hopped and gyrated among billows of multi-colored smoke. The sounds were high decibel, but the beat was good to dance to.

There weren't too many of us on the floor. Most of the club patrons were seated at the bar, among them a hefty couple that looked as if they had walked off the set of a Hell's Angels movie. The young woman was dark-haired and dour; the man wore a muscle T-shirt and had multiple tattoos.

Suddenly, the lead guitarist quit his prancing to announce that he was dedicating the next number to a biker couple who'd just come from their wedding. The tattooed man led his bride to the dance floor, followed by their friends— and us. As we danced past them, my husband called out, "Congratulations!"

The bridal couple looked astonished. And then smiled so sweetly. "Why thank you, sir, ma'am," the man said, softly.

His reaction put me in mind of a morning several years back when we'd been visiting our son in New York State. I'd taken a solitary walk, reveling in the abundance of birds and wildflowers, when I heard the roar of a motorcycle. Looking up, I saw a bushy-bearded, much-tattooed biker rumbling down the deserted, rural road.

I stepped to the side of the road to give him room, and he passed me in a whoosh of sound. Then he stopped his bike and got off.

I felt an adrenaline rush of pure panic as all of the horror stories I'd ever read rushed to my brain. Fear rooted me to the ground as that muscled, bearded figure advanced toward me and then detoured into a gully, where he commenced picking wildflowers. Seeing me stare, he shrugged sheepishly.

"My mom likes them," he growled.

From childhood, we're taught not to judge a book by its cover, and I believe this with all my heart. Sometimes, though, I slip up. Sometimes, when I come up against someone who doesn't conform to my ideas of good taste or behavior or belief, I begin to pigeonhole them. No matter that I shrink from the idea of stereotyping, I do the very thing I abhor.

But when I'm wrong—and so often I am—I'm both humbled and overjoyed that my core belief is right after all. And that there is beauty to be found in as many places as wildflowers grow.

MAUREEN CRANE WARTSKI, who makes her home in Raleigh, North Carolina, has taught high school English and writing, and she conducts writing workshops throughout the country. She has authored many young adult novels, including the award-winning *A Boat to Nowhere.* She has written short stories for *Boys' Life* magazine and for anthologies such as *Join In: Multiethnic Short Stories.* Ms. Wartski's book, *Yuri's Brush with Magic,* was recently published by Sleepy Hollow Books.

I Could Be Wrong

ALLAN BARGER

I believe in uncertainty. I believe that the four words "I could be wrong" should be etched above every school-room, house of worship, political assembly hall, and scientific laboratory. Uncertainty is an odd creed, but I find it deeply spiritual, combining humility and a deep respect for the mysteries of God and life. It's not an easy creed.

My conversion to uncertainty came from my life. As an evangelical Christian and a pastor, I spent years trying to reconcile my religious certainties with the certain fact that I was gay. I tried being not gay for almost twenty-five years only to find I had simply been wrong. It didn't help, and it didn't stop. In the process I hurt myself, and worse, I hurt others. Sometimes, no matter how certain I am, life and God hand me a different message. This was my hardest lesson in uncertainty. I didn't lose faith in God, but I certainly lost faith in certainty.

My commitment to uncertainty grows today because I see an appalling excess of certainty around me. It seems to me that certainty visits a great many evils upon the world. I see religions lose their humanity because they are certain they know divinity. Some commit acts of terror and others acts of political intolerance all in the name of God. I watch political certainties create inflexibility in the face of changing information and situations. I see scientific researchers sidelined by other scientists when their theories challenge the scientific orthodoxy—sidelined not because they lack sound evidence but because accepting their evidence means rethinking cherished certainties. It's human to resist uncertainty. I resist it myself. But when my certainties are in overdrive, I act as if the truth will die if I can't make you see it and then I can do terrible things. I need uncertainty to keep me humble.

Some ask me if it's crippling to always question myself. I find it uncomfortable, but not crippling. I act with more confidence if I know in my heart that I'm willing to abandon my certainties if the facts, or the outcomes, turn out wrong. Today, as a teacher and a research analyst, I have certain knowledge. I'm also pretty certain what I want for my children and grandchildren. I'm politically active because I hold certainties about human equality, democracy, and spirituality. I'm certain of a great many things, but I embrace uncertainty because it makes me a better person. I do make mistakes; it's part of being human. The real error is to be too certain to see my mistakes. Certainty becomes a prison for my mind. Humble uncertainty lets the truth emerge. That's why I believe in uncertainty—but I could be wrong.

ALLAN BARGER has worked as a research analyst with a nonprofit organization for nearly twenty years to reduce alcohol and drug problems in our society. He is also a parent of four amazing daughters and a grandparent of five extraordinary kids. Otherwise, Mr. Barger is a fairly normal and relatively boring guy.

Everyone Is Included

~∽~

CATHERINE MCDOWALL

I was not the least popular kid in my school, but I was probably in the bottom third. Hoping to elevate my social position a bit before high school, I begged my parents for permission to throw an eighth grade graduation party. To my utter shock and delight, they said yes.

I quickly drafted a list of invitees, including only my two best friends and fifteen or so of the most popular kids. But when I brought the list to my mother, she shook her head and explained, "No, you must invite the entire class or the party is off." Was she out of her mind? She rarely entertained her own friends, and now she was essentially forcing me to invite fifty or so young teens to our home?

Desperate for the party, I agreed to her terms. I spent an entire period of recess tracking down my classmates to pass out invitations. Perhaps not surprisingly, one of the last people I found was Maureen. Heavier and more awkward than most, Maureen typically spent recesses huddled in a corner trying to avoid the gaze of the other kids.

Maureen watched with apprehension as I approached her, no doubt fearing some put-down or teasing. I handed her the invitation and said, with a confident smile on my face, "I hope you can come, too!" I will never forget the look on her face as she took the invitation from me and offered a shy smile. At that moment, my mother's requirement to include everyone suddenly made perfect sense.

Some twenty-five years later, my own daughter, Sophie, started preschool in our neighborhood. At the parent meeting, we were informed of a rigid school rule: "Everyone is included." For example, kids were not permitted to exclude other kids from their play, kids could not discuss play dates that happened outside school hours that did not include everyone in the class, cubbies could only be used to distribute party invitations if the whole class was invited, and so forth.

Later, I overheard Sophie imploring her younger sister to let her join a game of Barbies by explaining, "Everyone is included, Jessica!" This poignant incident made me recall my experience learning this mantra, and made me reflect on how universally this tenet applied to almost every area of my life.

I throw parties that are too crowded and that require too much preparation and cleanup. My small kids can get overwhelmed by the number of children at their birthday parties. The softball team I organize for my office has too many players. A quick lunch at work with one friend quickly morphs into a group outing of eight or ten. But these events, with their boisterous chaos and unpredictability, are more enjoyable to me than many smaller events or intimate gatherings.

More significantly, in my work as a prosecutor, I believe that the law applies equally to everyone. The theft of a Ford Escort should be prosecuted with as much fervor as the theft of an Escalade. The rape of a prostitute deserves as much attention as the rape of a suburban mom. And the murder of a drug dealer should be pursued as heartily as the murder of a prominent public figure.

More broadly, my political and religious beliefs are founded on this tenet as well. Democracy is premised on the concept of "one person, one vote." Jesus taught us to "love your neighbor" and lived this commandment by loving enemies, tax collectors, prostitutes, foreigners, lepers, sinners, and even those who would harm him.

The vivid memory of Maureen's happiness at being included in my party helps to remind me of the value of this core belief and to apply it even when it may be difficult to do so. This is what I believe, and it guides me to this day: everyone is included.

CATHERINE MCDOWALL served the people of King County, Washington, as a deputy prosecutor for eleven years. She is currently taking a break from legal practice to raise her four children. Her husband inspires her and lovingly supports her need to include everyone.

A Lesson I Hold Dear

KARA GEBHART UHL

I believe I can be both honest and kind, even when the two seem to contradict.

Honesty often throws kindness for a loop. From telling someone there's food in their teeth all the way to telling someone you don't love them even though you know they love you—honest statements, although said with kind intentions, can often seem cruel.

I was sixteen years old, working at an amusement park, when I met Joe. He was older, had long, blond hair, and drove a motorcycle. The first time he called I smiled so hard my cheeks ached by the end of the conversation. He soon became my first boyfriend.

We dated the entire summer. By early fall he had said, "I love you." I said nothing. In the battle between kindness and honesty, honesty won.

In the months following our breakup, Joe left love notes on my bedroom windowsill. In college, he called twice. The first time we talked. The second time, he left a distraught voice mail. I returned his call and left a short message. I never heard from him again.

Several years later his sister called with news: Joe had committed suicide, months ago. Shortly before his death, his sister said, he had been diagnosed with bipolar disorder. Joe had written a few lines about me in his suicide note, but only now had she gathered the strength to call.

I thought about the first time Joe called, how my cheeks ached. The ache had returned—but this time, it was something much deeper. Not wanting to cry at work, I ran to my car and sobbed, both the finality of what he had done—and the fact that he had thought of me, even briefly, before he did it—sinking in. Once home, I reread his love letters to me. It was then I wanted so desperately to take back my silence, to tell him I loved him—not in a romantic sense, but in a you-deserve-to-live-a-long-life sense.

A few days later I went to a party on what would have been Joe's twenty-seventh birthday to celebrate his life. I met his family. I looked at old photos. I was intrigued to hear about the man he had become; we could have been great friends.

I hated myself for choosing honesty over kindness, for not writing more, for not calling more, for not doing more. I wasn't so bold as to think I could have fixed him. Rather, I was sad that I had to be unkind and tell him I didn't love him.

Several days later, worried I would never find peace, I reread what Joe wrote to me in his note: "How people should be . . . wonderful and I'm glad I had the time with her—still I have a wonderful feeling inside."

It was then I realized that Joe thought my honesty was kind. His words to me were his way of telling me so, his way of being honest—and kind—to me.

A year later, on what would have been Joe's twenty-eighth birthday, my husband and I put flowers by his grave. I thanked him for a lesson I'll always hold dear: I can be honest and still be kind.

KARA GEBHART UHL is a freelance writer and editor in her one-hundred-year-old foursquare in Fort Thomas, Kentucky. She blogs about raising her daughter and twin boys at www .pleiadesbee.com.

A Taste of Success

GEOFFREY CANADA

When I say I believe all children can learn, people some-times misunderstand.

Because I have been working with poor, minority children in Harlem for the last twenty-five years, some people think I am talking about good kids in bad environments—that if you give a bright kid from a poor family a good educational support system, he or she can succeed. That's absolutely true, but that's not what I mean.

You see, I truly believe that all kids can learn. I believe it, I've seen it, I've even tasted it.

Back in 1975 when I was coming out of Harvard Graduate School of Education, I worked in a summer camp in Ossipee, New Hampshire, for kids with the absolute toughest problems: emotionally disturbed kids, autistic kids, oppositional ADHD kids, kids that everyone—even their parents—had given up on.

One of the things that the staff and I did was cook with the kids. These children didn't know baking powder from table salt, but once they had eaten a warm biscuit out of the oven, smeared with melted butter and a drizzle of maple syrup, they were very motivated to learn how to make more.

Suddenly, kids who couldn't sit still or focus were carefully eyeballing ingredients as we measured them out, learning the simple math and spelling lessons we could slip in along the way. By the end of the summer, I remember parents breaking down and crying when they saw the progress their children had made.

The biscuits, by the way, were delicious, and I can still remember the taste of them today—and more important, I still remember the lesson they taught me: that if we, the adults, can find the right motivation for a child, there's hope for that child's education.

Today I run two charter schools and a series of educational programs, and we work with over ten thousand kids a year. I make sure that every single one of my staff understands that I don't accept excuses about kids not learning. You can't blame the kids. In my shop, if a child does not succeed, it means the adults around him or her have failed.

That's because the kids with the really tough problems are not going to suddenly start teaching themselves. I believe that we adults have to help them, and that starts with looking hard at each child, finding out what excites them, and exploiting that excitement shamelessly.

When I was growing up poor in the south Bronx, one of four boys raised by a single mom, I probably looked as if I was heading nowhere, hanging out on the street with my friends and getting into fights and trouble. And I would have ended up dead or in jail like many of my friends if it had not been for a couple of teachers and family members who saw something underneath my teenage tough-guy act. They spotted my fascination with reading, starting with *Green Eggs and Ham* and later with *Manchild in the Promised Land*, and they made sure I had great books to read.

Because of that, I have dedicated my life to going back into the most devastated communities in America and making sure kids like me don't get written off.

My first taste of success came way back at that summer camp in Ossipee, New Hampshire. It came with a plate of steaming hot biscuits that tasted so good I believe they could have brought a tear to your eye.

For nearly twenty years, GEOFFREY CANADA has been president and CEO of Harlem Children's Zone, a nonprofit organization providing education and support programs for poor families in Harlem. Mr. Canada is the author of *Fist Stick Knife Gun* and *Reaching Up for Manhood*.

A Grace of Silence

ANDREW FLEWELLING

I believe in silence.

Growing up in Wellesley, Massachusetts, my playground was the small, stone church where my father was minister. I remember riding my big-wheeled tricycle silently down the blue, carpeted center aisle and that the perfect refuge for hide-and-go-seek was under the altar cloth, because no one thought I would actually hide there. But it's the cool silence of that stone church that I remember the most. It was heady and gave me life. It was there that I could escape the scrutiny and expectations of being a child of color and the son of a preacher.

My white father brought his black wife and children to this blue-blooded community in 1968. Our world was changing. My experiences showed me that the attainability of the American Dream conflicted with the reality that my black skin seemed to tell people that I was still a threat, that I was base in the eyes of our free and equal society. I learned to step aside when passing white ladies on the sidewalk even while on my way to the elite private schools I attended.

In the silence of my father's church, beneath the sun-illumed stained glass, I could hear my own voice—it told me I was smart and helped me dream a life worth living. Outside the church, the deafening discord of society told me I was a subordinate person and someone to be feared.

As I got older, the noise of our civilization—television, movies, history, religion—began to dictate the way I thought I ought to live my life. Our cacophonous world not only drowned out my inner voice, it told other people how they should feel about me and those who look like me. I'm sorry they saw me as a monster. If only they could tune out the noise to hear my thoughts, the ones at my core, then they might realize how wrong they were about me. And maybe they would be free to see themselves in a new light as well.

When I was twenty-five, I found the strength to redis-cover my inner voice. It happened at the bedside of my dying father. In the soft quiet of our conversations, he told me to be my own man. He helped me recognize the noise of the world so I could learn to stop listening to it. He encouraged me to see my weaknesses and illuminate my strengths. For the first time since I was a child, I was able to hear the voice of my spirit. It told me what I value and how I ought to live my own life.

I believe in a silence that allows me to stop paying attention to the world around me and start listening to my heart. In the years since my father's death, I try daily to hear the silence amid the noise of career, children, war, recession, and success. Most days I find it as I walk with my daughters in the woods behind our home. It's the church of my adult life. I tell my girls about the grandfather they never knew and the lessons he gave me. I tell them how he saved my life.

I tell them I believe there is a voice inside all of us that needs to be heard.

ANDREW FLEWELLING moved to Vermont from Boston in 1997 after the death of his father, leaving behind a career in advertising to search for a quieter world in which to raise a family. Mr. Flewelling lives in the shadow of Mount Mansfield with his wife and two daughters and works for the University of Vermont.

Do Talk to Strangers

SABRINA DUBIK

I believe that we *should* talk to strangers. By engaging in unexpected, friendly conversation with strangers, our lives can be affected in ways that are extraordinary. I learned this valuable and life-changing experience during my sophomore year of college. I was a student and part-time waitress in Chicago, and I spent most of my time at work engaging in as little "real" conversation as possible. This was not done intentionally, but rather instinctively. Growing up, I was used to phrases such as, "Don't talk to strangers" and "Mind your own business." As a result, I didn't talk to unknown people at work, beyond taking orders and the occasional weather chat. Similarly, I never struck up a conversation on a three-hour plane flight or knew the name of the woman I rode the train with every day. But the process of keeping to myself ended in a life-changing way.

One night, a little old man, probably in his eighties, came in and sat in my section. I took his order and went on my way. But I noticed that he came in week after week and always sat at one of my tables. Slowly, I began having short conversations with my new guest. His name was Mr. Rodgers, but he insisted that I call him Don. I learned that he and his wife had gone to dinner and a movie every Saturday. Since she had died, he carried on the tradition alone. I began looking forward to him coming in and telling me his movie reviews. I also knew his order by heart: a half of a chicken salad sandwich, a cup of potato soup, and a bottle of Coors Light (which he never finished).

As the weeks went on I began to sit and really talk with Don. We talked about his wife, his days flying in the war, his son who had grown and moved away. Eventually, we began to talk about my ambitions—going to school, my new husband, and the anticipation of my future.

About four months after meeting Mr. Rodgers, I received a call at home from a nurse telling me that Don was in intensive care at Chicago's Mercy Hospital. He was experiencing complications from an emergency heart surgery and had begun to bleed internally. I immediately drove to the hospital to see him. The first thing he did was thank me for urging him to visit the doctor. At first I didn't know what he was referring to. Then I remembered that about three weeks earlier, Don was complaining about chest pains and I gave him the number for a doctor I knew. At the hospital, the nurses asked, "Are you his daughter?" and I replied, "No, I'm his waitress."

Since meeting Don, I have learned that strangers can become acquaintances, and even friends. I recently found myself really talking to customers at the restaurant. I have had a lot more fun, the time has gone by faster, and I have gotten to know some of the people I see on a regular basis. Don taught me that life can be much more enjoyable if I engage in friendly conversations. After all, I became more than just his waitress. I became his friend.

Since writing this essay when she was a student at Lewis University, SABRINA DUBIK has graduated and left behind her waitressing job to begin her career as an English teacher at Minooka High School. While teaching, she strives to inspire enthusiasm for literature, writing, and the art of living life.

Finding Our Common Ground

ROBIN MIZE

There was a big peace march in Washington a few years back. I watched as my husband made a sign to carry and my son painted slogans on a T-shirt. "Sure you don't want to come?" my husband asked me.

He knew that I was sympathetic to the cause. I felt just as strongly as he and all our friends, who were going, did. But I just couldn't go. I begged off, saying I wasn't comfortable with the crowds.

But the thing that made me uneasy wasn't just the number of people gathered there. It was the mob mentality of a large group of people who feel they are right, even if I agree with them. It was the absolutism lurking in the liberal ideals. To me it felt just as scary as any other kind of intolerance.

On the other hand, I know it takes a kind of fervor and belief to change things. But there is a fine line there, and somehow group protests, while I respect them, walk too close to that line for me. What scares me is the self-congratulatory, undiscriminating nature of the mob. I think of the French Revolution, I picture those Nazi rallies, and I fear the self-complacency of knowing that you are right.

I wonder if it has to do also with the fact that I come from a family in which the liberal is a rare bird. Four of my siblings are staunch conservative Republicans. I love them dearly, and the fact that these people whom I love are the evil enemy of the peace march gives me pause.

It forces me to accept a contradiction, knowing both things to be true. They are the enemy, but they are also my family. We do not agree, but I have to accept that they are thoughtful and compassionate people who have come to the opposite conclusion about how things should be. I must admit that it's hard for me to disagree so profoundly yet still respect and love them. Sometimes I wish I could agree with my siblings and not be troubled by these uncomfortable differences of opinion.

This brings me to what I believe: I believe we are all doing the best we can. The other side isn't any more ignorant or selfish than we are; they are not big business or big brother or the international monetary fund. They are just like me. I choose to respect their opinions, even as I disagree with them.

I am grateful that my children must accept this diversity, too. They can't just dismiss the other side as evil. They are forced to love the enemy because the enemy is their loved one. The love came first.

It seems to me that here in my family is an essential element of our democracy: we agree to disagree. Our ability not only to accept, but to respect, our differences is our common ground.

Licensed marriage and family therapist ROBIN MIZE works with individuals, couples, and groups. Before studying counseling, Ms. Mize received a PhD in drama from the University of California, Santa Barbara. She lives with her family in Takoma Park, Maryland.

Bus Chick's Manifesto

CARLA SAULTER

When I was in third grade, I started riding the Metro bus alone. At first, I was allowed to ride to school only, but eventually my parents extended my privileges to include my favorite childhood haunts: Grandma's apartment, Pike Place Market, and in the summer Seattle Center. Back then the bus symbolized independence. It gave me a power rare among my eight-year-old peers: the ability to get around the city without the assistance of an adult.

By the time I turned sixteen, a new power beckoned—a form of transportation that was available on demand and did not require an umbrella or an extra pair of gloves.

Like most young Americans, I believed the auto industry's propaganda: that a car was required for my transition to adulthood. For the next ten years—except for a short time in college when I found myself unable to afford a personal vehicle—I left the bus behind.

But then I accepted a job at a software company based fifteen miles outside the city. During my commutes, I became more aware of the negative impact of car culture: pollution, sprawl, isolation, and fatalities. I began to question my right to subject the earth and my beloved city to the impact of my choices. So, I returned to my roots and began riding the bus to work. Eventually, I was using my car so rarely that I decided to try living without one. I sold my lovely silver coupe in March 2003 and have used the bus as my primary form of transportation ever since.

Riding the bus isn't always fun. I don't like riding on rainy days, when the floor is slippery and the windows so fogged up you can't see your stop. I don't like standing when the bus is crowded. I don't like drivers who ride the brakes. I don't like practical hairstyles or sensible shoes. Despite these occasional inconveniences, I will never go back to driving, because this I believe:

I believe in sitting next to my neighbors, in saying, "How you doing today?" and "Nice weather, isn't it?" I believe in feeling the sun on my skin, in breathing fresh air and moving my body. I believe in eavesdropping. I believe in novels you can't put down. I believe in businesspeople and teenage lovers, middle-aged gossips and giggling toddlers. I believe in watching and listening. I believe in naps. I believe in the camaraderie that develops among riders late at night, when the smooth-voiced driver plays jazz loud enough for everyone to enjoy.

I believe in clean air, in keeping cities dense and vibrant, and in protecting our remaining farmland and forests. I believe in the beauty of Puget Sound and the majesty of Mount Rainier. I believe that human life is sacred, that the world's resources should be shared, and that every choice matters.

I believe that change is possible—if all of us ride.

Freelance writer CARLA SAULTER, aka Bus Chick, blogs about transit riding on her website, buschick.com. She serves on Seattle's Transit Master Plan Advisory Board. Ms. Saulter and her husband and two children still enjoy life without a personal vehicle.

Right Now Matters

SAMANTHA JACOBS

After seventeen years of getting up and going to school every morning, I ended my formal education and entered the notorious "real world." My mother warned me when she said, "You are about to enter a really weird time in your life, and I can't prepare you for it. Just be aware." Boy, was she ever right.

Eager to get far away from my college town in Tennessee, I moved back to my native St. Louis and landed a job as a nanny for a wealthy and extremely likable family. As far as nanny work goes, I struck gold. Yet I was uncomfortable with being a college graduate and working as a less-cool version of Mary Poppins. While my friends were going off to law school or getting married or doing the daily grind in glamorous cities, I was concerned about strategically placing Eggo waffles in the toaster so they didn't burn, while maintaining that crispy grid.

Reason told me that what I was doing mattered, providing care and protection for two young children, but my insecurities thought otherwise. I began to blame myself for my current state of affairs. I made the decision to get this job, to flee Tennessee, and to not invest any time in looking for more "challenging" work. Needless to say, it was turning into that weird time my mother warned me about.

While torturing myself with feelings of insignificance about my job, I tried to find worth in other things, like running, sporadic blogging, weekend getaways, dying my hair, etc., but nothing seemed to fulfill me. Then I had one of those "aha!" moments where everything becomes unmistakably clear. I was playing outside with my little charges when one of them came up and said, "You're so great. You don't even have to play with us but you do it anyway. Our other nannies never did that. We love you!"

I was floored. Not only did I underestimate their ability to be so gracious, but they made me realize that it's truly not about what life hands you but what you do with it. That whole "making lemonade out of lemons" thing really hit home for me on this one. I could easily just patrol these girls, make sure they don't run out in the street or draw all over the walls, but I don't. I play with them. I make my life a part of theirs and vice versa. And together, we have perfected the fine art of Eggo toasting. How many people can say that?

So what do I believe in? I believe that self-worth is where you find it and that the most beautiful form of self-worth occurs when you maximize the amount of love you share with the world, no matter how mundane or humble the circumstances may be. I believe that just because you have a college degree doesn't mean you need a job with a BlackBerry. And most important, I believe in lemonade.

SAMANTHA JACOBS is working toward her master's in art education in St. Louis, Missouri, and is looking forward to becoming a career art educator. Although no longer a nanny, Ms. Jacobs does continue to babysit and eat Eggo waffles on a regular basis.

Seeing with the Heart

STEPHANIE DISNEY

Looking at my daughter, the clerk behind the counter asks, "What is she?" Since this is not the first time I have heard this question, the stored-up, smart-aleck answers swirl through my mind. Instead, understanding that I am my daughter's role model for handling life issues, I stifle the negativity and respond, "She's beautiful, and smart, and well behaved, too."

The clerk says, "Oh," and glances at me, wondering if I just didn't understand the question, and I smile because I understood the question right away, but I am only just now beginning to understand the real answer: that family is defined by bonds much deeper than birth, or skin color, or genetics. Like anyone lucky enough to experience "found" love, I believe that family is defined only by the heart.

I met my daughter, Rudy, while working as an audiologist at the Commission for Children with Special Health Care Needs. She was a small, quiet, noncommunicative two-and-a-half-year-old—and my heart recognized her immediately.

I am the whitest of white women, and my daughter is some indefinable combination of all that is beautiful from at least three races: curly, dark hair; petite features; freckles; a golden tan skin tone; one blue eye and one brown. If her race had only one name it would be perfection.

My daughter and I share so much in common it never occurs to me that others might not see us as a family. That's why I was startled the first time a stranger inquired about my daughter's race and our relationship. I had forgotten that we didn't look alike. The next time I was asked, I politely explained that we are mother and daughter and that Rudy's race is unknown. The twentieth time somebody asked about my daughter's race and our relationship, I explained why the questions were inappropriate. The fortieth time someone asked, I just pretended not to hear.

Now, after much time to reflect about the purpose of these questions, I understand. I understand that everyone wants love and acceptance. And these are such rare gifts that when people see them freely demonstrated, they are compelled to seek the source.

Recently, Rudy surprised me when a white-haired lady, standing right beside us, asked if I was her mother. Rudy threw the lady a disbelieving glance and said, "Well, she helps me with multiplication, fixes my hair, kisses me, and we both have freckles on our noses—who else could she be?"

When Rudy asks me to explain why people need to ask questions like that, I tell her not to worry, it's the answers that really matter. The questions of race and family can be complicated to be sure, but I believe all of the answers can be found by seeing people first with the heart.

Clinical audiologist STEPHANIE DISNEY has led hearing screening programs for newborns and has served adults with mental disabilities and children with special health care needs.

Speak Now or Forever Hold Your Peace

DANI WEATHERS

When my dad died, we weren't there to say good-bye. He was alone on a Colorado road riding that stupid motorcycle he just had to have. When he died, I felt like I died, too.

I was diagnosed with manic depression and post-traumatic stress disorder shortly after my dad died on August 6, 2006, hit by a woman in a car. His death left me numb and empty. Desperate to feel something—to feel anything—I resorted to cutting myself. I thought if I could feel the pain of sharp objects digging into my skin, then I was still alive. Soon I was addicted to self-injury.

My depression and my cutting became too much for what was left of my family. My mother and brother seemed too distant to save me from my misery. We became strangers in the house we'd lived in since I was eight. I came to hate them, and in hating them, I felt more alone than before. My cutting grew more frequent.

Eventually, I felt scared of the person I had become; I didn't want to cut anymore, but I was terrified of what would happen if I didn't. The people closest to me were weary of my ongoing battles, too. At one point, a former boyfriend shouted at me, "It happened four years ago! Get over it already! Just move on!"

His words stunned me like a slap in the face, stopping me from grabbing anything sharp. Although I disagreed that I should "get over" my father's death, I realized I couldn't continue to let cutting and depression control my life. After all, Dad wouldn't want me to hurt myself this way. I also saw how unfair it was to depend on my incredibly patient friends to clean up my messes. After years of trying to mend my grief by cutting, I was finally ready for the real process of healing to begin.

It hasn't been easy to share my tale. When people hear about my depression, they pity me or, worse, think I'm crazy. But what would remaining quiet achieve? My silence won't heal my wounds—in fact, it nearly cost me the last bit of life I kept buried under my pain and loss.

So I say to the world, I have depression, and I am a recovering cutter. I believe I am worth something, and I don't want to fear what other people think of me. I want to live another day, because I believe that this scary, horrible, and yet awesome world is worth fighting for. My visible and invisible wounds are signs of my strength and the trials I've struggled to survive. And I hope that by telling my story I can help other people who share this addiction.

Today, my smiles are sincere, my laughs genuine. Today I am a new girl, a phoenix reborn from the ashes of all of the tragedy and struggle that had been my life. Today I believe I am alive.

And Dad, wherever you are now, know that I love you.

DANI WEATHERS is a charismatic human specimen, but she still has demons of her own. She is a sophomore studying English at Ohio State University. Ms. Weathers aspires to be a future teen fiction author, but for now she is content with learning to reenjoy life with her friends, family, and her four wonderful cats.

The Triumph of Kindness

JOSH STEIN

I believe that when people come together, it's a beautiful thing. And when someone who can't do something tries to do it and everyone else helps, that is a great moment.

One beautiful sunny day, I had a Little League baseball game. At the time it was very important to me, and I was really focused on doing well, as were the other seven-year-olds. It was our last game of the season, and we were all trying to have fun and to end it with a bang the best we could.

As the game progressed the score got close. When we had our final chance to win at the end of the last inning, it was my turn to bat. I looked over at my coach, who was talking to my dad about something—probably the stock market or something like that. As I stepped into the batter's box, my coach called me back to the dugout. He asked me a strange yet interesting question. He asked if it would be all right if my brother hit for me.

My brother wasn't on the team. He had never even played baseball due to his disability. He couldn't stand, and he certainly couldn't hit. But I responded very maturely for a kid my age. "Of course he can hit for me," I said. I was still puzzled as to how, though. Thoughts ran through my mind, such as: Would the kids make fun of him? Would he hit the ball?

As my dad carried him to the plate, I realized that without his wheelchair he would have to be held up. The joy on his face couldn't be traded for anything in the world. Just being on the field gave him all the happiness he needed. What will the other kids think? I wondered.

I heard someone call out, "C'mon, hit it outta here." Then came another, "You can do it!" These words of acceptance showed me how great the moment really was. On the first swing, which was pretty much my dad holding Sam's hands around the bat and my dad swinging, he—or they—hit the ball. The kids on the other team did something amazing then, something seven-year-olds should never know how or why to do. But in the spur of the moment, these seven-year-olds did. They purposely overthrew the ball. Three times.

Sam had hit his first and only home run. And as my dad carried him around the bases, I knew this memory would stick with me and everyone else there forever.

I've seen it with my own eyes. When people come together, it's a beautiful thing.

JOSH STEIN is a ninth grader at Hewlett High School in Hewlett, New York. He enjoys playing tennis, basketball, and golf and hanging out with his brothers.

Time to Walk the Dog

BETSY BUCHALTER ADLER

I believe in walking the dog.

I also believe in flossing my teeth, practicing the piano, and eating five servings of fruits and vegetables a day, but those things can be ignored. The dog cannot be ignored.

The dog stands in the doorway, polite but implacable, waiting for me to clip on his leash. He couldn't care less about my deadlines and duties. He knows, and I know, that the walk is the thing.

Walking the dog is not aerobic exercise. It's a meander. We stop periodically so the dog can read the latest smells with his long, elegant collie nose. We walk to the park or the bakery or just around the neighborhood. The dog is amenable to all of these destinations. He's outside. I'm on the other end of the leash. Life is good.

I could say I got the dog for exercise or to get myself out of the house or to have an excuse for my husband and me to make up silly songs, the way we did when our kids—all grown up now—were too young to roll their eyes at us.

But in fact I got the dog to have an anchor in the ordinary world of sights and smells, outside the words and laws that are the tools of my legal practice. Lawyers are surrounded by rules, agreements, promises made and broken. We parse words to determine who is legally bound to do what. Then we try to connect those obligations to the facts in front of us in order to solve somebody's problem. It's all too easy to focus on work to the exclusion of, well, meandering.

The dog forces me to meander. I have to stop trying to make facts and rules behave themselves and focus on what's going on right here, right now, like the ruby-throated hummingbird zooming around my neighbor's Mexican sage. I would have missed it completely if the dog hadn't stopped and stared. I would have gone right past that tiny red sock in the middle of the sidewalk, kicked off by some passing baby in a stroller, if the dog hadn't pounced on it and carried it away in dogly triumph.

Walking the dog makes me lighten up and pay attention, not to what's in my own head but to the unexpected small delights of the actual world. The dog gets me out of the four walls—work, clock, computer, phone—and into the land of smells and colors and serendipities. He reminds me of everything I can't control and don't need to.

Some religions elevate walking to the level of meditation, but I don't reach that high. I believe in modest miracles: the hummingbird, the red sock, the fact that my middle-aged body still works. I believe in paying attention. I believe in meandering. I believe it's time to take the dog for a walk.

BETSY BUCHALTER ADLER is a writer, a birder, a philanthropic adviser, and a lawyer for nonprofit organizations and their donors. A graduate of Cowell College at the University of California, Santa Cruz, she lives with her husband of forty-two years and their dog, Ollie, a short-haired collie, in Northern California and Manhattan.

Yankee Go Home

RITA BARRETT

It wasn't shaping up to be my ideal Christmas Eve. I had spent much of the day fighting the urge to cry, and my spirits were low as I boarded the train with my two best friends.

The train's destination was León, Spain, but I wished it could transport me to Portland, Oregon, USA. I was studying at a Spanish college and had planned to spend Christmas with a friend who was studying in Austria and another who had come over from the United States for the holiday. Our tour of Spain over the break sounded exciting as we planned the itinerary in our letters, but on the twenty-fourth of December our adventure dulled in comparison to being home with our families.

On the train, we talked about all that had happened since we last saw one another in September. Our English marked us as foreigners on a train carrying excited Spaniards home for la Nochebuena, Christmas Eve, with their families. A few seats away, a Spanish university student stared at us. Reaching into his scanty English vocabulary, he wrote a greeting in the steam on his window: "Yankee Go Home."

Oh, if only we could go home! After contemplating his sentiment for a moment, I called out to the young man in Spanish, "You want us to leave?"

Surprised to hear me speak his language, he responded with the expected political opinions. I'd already discovered the resentment some Spaniards felt toward the American military bases in their country, and I wasn't surprised when he raised that issue. My Spanish wasn't perfect, but I translated for my friends as we shared our opinions. As we talked, the Spaniard seemed surprised that our convictions didn't match the stereotype he had of Americans. The young man finally conceded that perhaps not all Americans were out to dominate the world, and we began laughing and enjoying our conversation.

Our new companion's stop came before León, and he said good-bye as he gathered his things and walked toward the exit. Suddenly he stopped and turned back to his seat.

Wiping off the phrase on the window with his jacket sleeve, he replaced it with a single English word: "Welcome."

When I think about that homesick Christmas Eve, the encounter on the train seems so appropriate for the season of "peace on earth, good will toward men." How amazing that just a few minutes of talking with ordinary Americans shattered the stereotypes the young Spaniard held.

The following summer the friend who had studied in Austria and I traveled through Europe, making new friends in several countries. We stayed with a goat herder's family in Sicily, ate at the home of a medical school student in Florence, chatted with people in France, and helped build a church in Germany. What was our secret to meeting these people? Well, between the two of us, my friend and I could speak or at least stumble around in five languages. Not only did getting to know us change their views of Americans, but our own stereotypes crumbled as we got to know people.

I believe that learning another language gives one the amazing power to break down cultural walls and bring people together. I have found that nothing warms the soul of a native more than hearing a visitor attempt to communicate in his language. Speaking another's language shows interest and respect for that person and his country. It says, "I value your culture, and I don't expect you to do all the work in this relationship." If we want world peace, I believe a good place to start is to learn to speak the world's languages.

RITA BARRETT teaches Spanish to high school students in Portland, Oregon. Ms. Barrett hopes that by learning a new language, her students will grow up to be people who erase "Go Home" and replace it with "Welcome."

The Courage to Change the Things I Can

MARK OLMSTED

I believe in picking up trash.

I've always hated litter; in fact, I once walked out in the middle of a date because my companion threw a wrapper on the sidewalk. In my opinion, it's the most preventable and stupid of the world's sins, and it is all the more infuriating because it has no advocates. For example, although I am also against corporal punishment, there are people who would readily argue that it is a useful and necessary form of discipline. No one ever defends littering—even its practitioners.

Yet I am not one to throw stones. For the first several years of this millennium, I was a drug addict who sold crystal meth to support my habit. My buying and selling certainly contributed to a lot of toxic waste created by meth labs. After nine months of prison and a commitment to sobriety, I knew I had to make amends.

After moving to the enclave of Little Armenia in Los Angeles, my first reaction to the trash-filled streets was to say a well-known prayer: "God grant me the serenity to accept the things I cannot change, the courage to change the things I can, and the wisdom to know the difference." As I walked my dog every day, I thought the litter was something I just had to accept. After all, what was I supposed to do? Pick it up?

Then one day, I decided to do just that. With a leap of faith, I went down to Home Depot, bought myself an E-Z Reacher, and just like that, I started plucking the empty cigarette packs, soda cans, fast-food packaging, coffee containers, newspapers, Styrofoam cups, and just about anything you can think of into plastic grocery bags. For over five years now, I have filled at least four bags every morning, one for each block of my dog-walking route. Sometimes, I do it again on different streets in the afternoon, especially if I'm having a bad day.

I believe in picking up trash because it's taught me that you can't assume to know the difference between the things you must accept and the things that you can change— you have to think about it. It's taught me to question the premise of all sorts of assumptions I had previously made, from the idea that the only possible reaction to traffic is anger and frustration to the belief that I was a hopeless addict who couldn't possibly get sober.

Every morning, picking up trash is my answer to the questions: How can I be of service today? What do I have the courage to change? And every night, no matter how much the day didn't seem to go my way, I can fall asleep counting the bags of trash I've picked up, comforted that in this lifetime I've been able to find one thing to do that's unarguably, unambiguously good.

MARK OLMSTED is a former drug addict who undertook keeping his neighborhood clean as part of his recovery regimen. He conducts lectures titled "The Six Spiritual Principles of Picking Up Trash" from his base in Hollywood, California, where he still picks up bags of litter every day. His website is www.trashwhisperer.com.

To Hear Your Inner Voice

CHRISTINE TODD WHITMAN

If I have learned nothing else during the course of my life, I've learned to listen to my inner voice. Everyone has one. We call it different things: our moral compass, a gut feeling, following our heart. Whatever we name it, we should always pay attention to it. It makes us who we are.

Nine years ago I was in the second year of my second term as governor of New Jersey. I loved that job, and I was working hard to make what would be my last term, due to term limits, as productive as my first.

Toward the end of that term a U.S. Senate seat opened for New Jersey, and I quickly came under intense pressure to throw my hat into the ring. As soon as I said yes, I knew I should have said no.

Deep down, I knew I didn't want to run for the Senate. I could do much more as my state's chief executive than I could in Washington, where I would be just one-one-hundredth of one-half of one-third of the federal government. And the idea of appealing to special interests for the money I would have to raise didn't sit well with me. My inner voice was telling me loud and clear, "Don't do it." I didn't listen.

In the end, all it took was one trip to Washington, D.C., as a Senate candidate to know that I just couldn't see this through. So I dropped out of the race, returned the money that we had raised, and went back to being governor. My aborted campaign wasn't one of my finer moments. But it reaffirmed my belief in following my inner voice.

A far more personal moment came when my inner voice told me to do something and I didn't listen. It was the night before my brother's third heart surgery, when I visited him in the hospital. After a walk down the hall and a light talk about our children, it was time to leave. As I saw him lying in his hospital bed I had an overwhelming urge to give him a hug and wish him luck. That kind of emotional display was out of character for us, and I thought it might tell him I was worried, so I didn't do it. My brother didn't survive the surgery.

As I look back I know that most of the mistakes I have made have come when I didn't listen to myself, when I didn't trust my instincts.

There is so much coming at us every day that life can get very confusing, but, as I have always told my children, there is only one person with whom you go to bed every night and get up with every morning, and that is you. Sometimes you stop paying attention to yourself. I believe you need to listen, carefully, to hear your inner voice. And then you have to do what it says.

From 1994 to 2001, CHRISTINE TODD WHITMAN served as the first female governor of New Jersey. She was also head of the U.S. Environmental Protection Agency from 2001 to 2003. Ms. Whitman now leads the Whitman Strategy Group, a consulting firm that focuses on energy and environmental issues.

Keep It Real

∽

ROSE EIESLAND FOSTER

My philosophy of life sure isn't the same as it was, say, twenty-two years ago. In 1983, I intended to complete college and become a professional of some sort, fully independent of anyone else, fully self-supporting. Not answering to another and being self-sufficient meant I would be a success. Nice clothes, nice car, nice "stuff"—these were things I felt would grant me a successful life.

But genetics and circumstance toiled with me. My body developed cancer twice before I hit forty, nearly killing me. Two of my adult siblings died from a rare kidney disease. I literally bumped into the man who would become my lover, best friend, husband, and father of my two children. Love leveled me into a state of the highest of highs, and, ultimately, the lowest of lows. My heart, unseen by others, was in for a workout. I discovered that loving and loss are always connected. I hate that. I "lost" my lover to mental illness; I "lost" my sister, brother, and mother to physical illness; and I "lost" the youthful appearance of health as my body adjusted to losing a breast. I had a nice car, some nice clothes, and a nice house. But, on the inside, things looked pretty grim.

Burying my forty-year-old husband, I made a vow to myself and to my two amazing children—that I would spend the rest of my life "being real." Being real means letting my hem show, letting the tears flow, and telling the truth about things. It no longer means anything to me how things look. All that matters to me now is how things are. Being real means telling the truth, no matter how harsh and stark that might be. It means writing down my actual weight, going without makeup for days at a time, letting my arms flap in the breeze. It means telling my dad every single time I see him that I love him. It means saying aloud how much I miss my husband, or my sister, or my brother. And being real means asking for help.

Where did self-sufficiency and smooth skin and nice nails go? I always thought that asking for help meant I was deficient in some way. "If there is anything I can do, please let me know," many have said to me. But instead of politely declining an invitation to dinner for fear I might start crying in the middle of dessert, I go. If someone wants to know how I am, I tell them. "Today, I thought about my husband eight hundred times and ate two ice cream cones for lunch." And, then, something happens. The person who asks me how I am says, "Well, me too." Tears shed during dinner are met with an embrace and a long talk after.

So my philosophy of life now is just three words long: keep things real. And it hasn't let me down yet.

ROSE EIESLAND FOSTER is pursuing her graduate degree in social work and lives in Lawrence, Kansas. She helps counsel others who have lost loved ones to suicide, and she hopes to secure employment counseling others who struggle with issues related to grief. Her son, Sam, is attending art school in Wisconsin, and her daughter is a junior in high school.

Important Strangers

LESLIE GUTTMAN

The bookstore was warm and cozy. It was packed, maybe because people didn't realize the rain had stopped. I was on a lunch break. I got a weird feeling. Someone was looking at me.

I looked up. A woman with long, black hair about five feet away quickly looked back down at the book she was leafing through. I looked down, too. More people came in the door. The gust of air that followed them smelled clean, as if it had been freshly laundered.

I glanced up again at the dark-haired woman in time to see her slip a book into her satchel and walk off. I hesitated and then walked after her.

"Pssst," I said, pointing at the satchel. Up close, I saw that she was about thirty and probably homeless. Her khaki parka was filthy, her hair matted. The satchel was bursting with her belongings. She gave me a sorrowful look. Then she handed me the book and ran off.

The manager came up, having seen what had happened. The book was a journal designed for someone who was grieving. Someone like me. It was beautifully bound, the paper creamy and heavy. It had space to write the answers to statements like: "I miss the way you . . ." and "It's hard for me to be without you when I . . ."

"She's been wanting that book," said the manager. "She comes in all the time and looks at it. Sometimes, she puts it on hold, but then she never gets it."

Dammit! I thought. Why did I have to be such a Goody Two-shoes? When will I learn to mind my own business? Why didn't I just let her steal it?

I ran out of the store. It was raining again. I caught up with her a block away. "Did you just lose someone?" I said.

"My grandmother," she said. "I used to talk to her every day, and I miss her so much I can't stand it." I told her about my stepdad, who had just passed away. His kindness had helped knit our family together for eighteen years.

I told her to wait a second. I knew I was now in a Buddhist fable in which nothing is an accident. When I came back and handed her the book, we both stood on the curb and wept.

For the first time since my stepdad died, I felt understood—as only a stranger can understand you, without inadequacy or regret. Up until then, I had felt alone in my grief. I was reluctant to turn to my family because they were grieving, too. The love of friends had not been able to dilute my sorrow.

But because the grieving thief and I didn't know each other, I had no expectations of whether I would be understood in my grief and no fear of being disappointed if I wasn't. Since we wouldn't see each other again, I could be emotional without being embarrassed or scared it would drive someone away.

I believe life, or God, or whatever you want to call it, puts people in our path so that they can help us, or we them—or both. This encounter made me want to stay open to the chance meeting with an important stranger, to the possibility of unplanned symmetry that is luminous and magical.

LESLIE GUTTMAN is an independent journalist who lives in Lexington, Kentucky, where she grew up. She worked at the *San Francisco Chronicle* for over a decade and is the author of *Equine ER: Stories from a Year in the Life of an Equine Veterinary Hospital* published by Eclipse Press.

My Parents as Friends

BHAVANI G. MURUGESAN

I believe in living with my parents. It's been almost two years since I came to live at home. I never meant to stay this long—not after years of boundless freedom at schools, stumbling out of cabs at four in the morning, leaving kitchen sinks filled with week-old dishes.

Coming home was meant to be a short, inexpensive stint until I passed the bar, fixed my broken bank account, and moved to the Big City. Today, at twenty-seven, long after my bank account is softly purring, I continue to live with my parents. I have come to rediscover them in ways that my teenage mind would not allow—as adults and as friends with flaws and oddities very simply their own. And sometimes, even mine.

Growing up, I remember my father as a silent, stern man—not the sort of person around whom one could laugh. As a teenager arriving in America, knowing nothing, I wanted a father who could explain the human journey. In college, when friends called home for advice, I would slump into a deep melancholy for what I did not have.

Then one night after my move back home, I overheard my father on the telephone. There was some trouble. Later, Appa shared the problem with me. Apparently my legal training had earned me some privileges in his eyes. I talked through the problem with Appa, analyzing the motives of the people involved and offering several negotiation strategies.

He listened patiently before finally admitting, "I can't think like that. I am a simple man."

Appa is a brilliant scientist who can deconstruct the building blocks of nature. Yet *human* nature is a mystery to him. That night I realized that he was simply not skilled at dealing with people, much less the turbulence of a conflicted teenager. It's not in his nature to understand human desires.

And so, there it was—it was no one's fault that my father held no interest in human lives while I placed great importance in them. We are at times born more sensitive, wide-eyed, and dreamy than our parents and become more compassionate, curious, and idealistic than them. Appa perhaps never expected me for a child. And I, who knew Appa as an intelligent man, had never understood that his intelligence did not cover all of my passions.

So what do I believe? I believe that coming home has saved me hours of wrestling with my angst on a shrink's couch. It has saved me years of questioning and confusion. It has saved my friends from carrying my destructive emotional baggage. I now see my parents as people who have other relationships than just Appa and Amma, relationships that shape and define them. I now overlook their many quirks—quirks that once seemed like monumental whims directed at me and me alone. I have forgiven myself for my picked-up habits, my homegrown eccentricities.

Best of all, I now know my parents as friends: people who ask me for advice; people who need my support and understanding. And I've come to see my past clearer. After our move from India, my parents have become my only link to a great part of my heritage. Knowing them makes me secure in where I come from and where I'm going.

BHAVANI G. MURUGESAN is a litigator in Sacramento, California. Every day she pauses to relish one small moment of happiness, whether it be a baby's head bobbing over his father's shoulder, the rustling of leaves, or a clean and empty sink at the end of the day—a sight still rare in her life.

A Good Neighborhood

JEFF NIXA

I live in a bad neighborhood.

At least that's what people said about it. "Cottage Grove Avenue," said a friend. "That's a bad neighborhood." A co-worker said, "I wouldn't buy there. There's no resale value." One mother was appalled. "Don't you want your kids to go to a good school?" Even our real estate agent sat me down and said, "Think about your wife's safety."

Soon the fear began to sink in. I called friends who lived there and asked, "Do you feel safe?" They laughed. "Have you been talking to real estate people again?" They invited us to dinner, in the bad neighborhood.

As we drove up, I scanned the streets as if on a recon mission in Fallujah. But our friends welcomed us in, poured wine, gave thanks, and passed homemade bread. After dessert they brought out crime statistics on a map from local police.

Sure enough, in the blocks surrounding us a vacant house had been vandalized. Drugs confiscated from a woman. A man passed out in a yard. This was as bad as—college.

Then I noticed the same symbols dotting the rest of the city: robberies, rapes, domestic violence. That month burglaries and auto thefts were worse in a wealthy suburb.

That's when I realized that all of those warnings really weren't about crime, real estate values, or schools. They were code words white folks like me use to signal "low-income people of color"—a perfectly concealed racist weapon, hidden deep in the anxious beliefs of my own friends and colleagues.

I believe sometimes the truth does set people free. So we bought the house on Cottage Grove.

That was seven years ago. No one told me that the day we moved in, a pack of joyful kids would run over to meet our kids. That our historic house cost less than a minivan. About Demetrius, raising his nieces while their mother is doing time. About Jose and Maria's burrito place. And Mike, the ponytailed Harley biker who one day stepped out directly in front of a speeding car and yelled "Hey," to the startled driver, slamming his fist on the hood, "there's kids around here!"

In my "bad" neighborhood, we sit on front porches, hear the neighbor girls' jazz double-dutch jump rope riffs, and buy snow cones on hot days out of an old guy's shopping cart.

Sure, there are nuisances here: litter, alley dogs, clutter in yards. But danger? I've learned that stupid behavior is color blind, and bullets prefer alcohol and drug deals over law-abiding citizens any day.

I love my new neighborhood—it balances my life, shows me real color, and saves me from things far worse than litter or a stolen Subaru—like the blindness and coded racism of privilege.

JEFF NIXA has lived with his family in South Bend's Near Northwest neighborhood since 1996. He is a commentator for *Michiana Chronicles* on local public radio station WVPE. Mr. Nixa has a law degree, and his careers have included hospital chaplain, massage therapist, and counselor. His interests include sea kayaking, bike commuting, running, woodworking, and landscaping. He is currently completing an apprenticeship with a Cherokee healer and plans to offer classes on urban shamanism to help people open their hearts and honor the earth.

Believing in People

REBECCA KLOTT

I believe in the power of children.

As a psychotherapist for children in a small rural county I have watched, for ten years, children overcome some of the worst types of abuse and neglect one can imagine. I have watched children carry Sesame Street–character lunchboxes into my tiny office, sit in a chair twice the size of their tiny bodies, and tell me how they are surviving while their daddies cook meth in the bathtub to make money so they can have electricity the next month. I have sat with teenagers of alcoholic parents as they try to figure out a way to help their parents get better. I have visited homes where the walls appear to move as cockroaches take over the house of a five-year-old boy.

Children can and do survive. Recently, a young woman I had treated in the beginning of my career saw me in a local grocery store. She was an angry, aggressive sixteen-year-old when I first met her. She'd been sexually molested, beaten, abandoned, and placed into foster care before I knew her. She'd seen scores of mental health professionals and had no use for the lot of us. She had scowled at me, called me names, and told me I had no business talking to her. And she'd been right. I was young, inexperienced, and knew nothing that would take away the grief she knew. So, when I saw her ten years later, my stomach lurched with regrets about all of the things I knew then that I couldn't give her when we first met.

I wanted to disappear, to get lost in a shelf full of potato chips. But she came straight to me and shoved a clean, soft hand my way, and a smile spread across her wide lips.

"Thank you," she said.

"For what?" It was all I could say, as I knew I had done nothing for this girl-woman.

"For believing in me."

And she was right, I had believed more in *her* than I had in myself.

She went on to tell me about how much this belief had bothered her, haunted her, angered her, and healed her. And how she couldn't get away from it. She had finished high school, late she told me, but she'd finished. She was working part-time and taking classes to become a massage therapist. She had one child. And this was what she said she felt I'd helped her with the most: believing in this child, her child, as her parents had not believed in her.

I believe that believing in a person can help them believe in themselves. I believe we must, *must* keep believing even when we want to stop, to turn away in disgust and despair. Because, even when we think there is no hope for a child, they might show up next to the Pop-Tarts in a local store and remind you of their power.

At the time this essay was written, REBECCA KLOTT was working in a community mental health setting. Since that time, she has returned to school and is working on her doctoral degree. Ms. Klott lives with her husband and daughter in Michigan.

Becoming Friends

❧

LARRY CHASTON

This I believe: when people find their commonalities they can get along and become friends.

In 2002, I was stationed at a firebase in Afghanistan. Al-Qaeda had invaded the country a decade before and had imposed their fundamentalist ideas on the local Pashtoon people. We were there to gain back their freedom. I knew we had to win their hearts as well as their minds—but this would not be easy. As Christians (Catholic, Mormon, and Protestant), we were considered infidels.

In January of that year, al-Qaeda destroyed the mosque where the villagers worshiped. Our unit offered to help rebuild the mosque, but our senior interpreter, Abdul Hajji, discouraged the plan. He did not want infidels building their place of worship.

Abdul and I discussed other possibilities, including keeping infidels, us, away from the mosque, especially after it was built. We could accidently desecrate it with thoughtless acts. I told Abdul we were the same: we both believed in strong family, we both honored the laws of Moses, and we both prayed to the same God.

Abdul asked, "Do you pray to Allah?"

I responded, "I pray to the God of Abraham." Abdul nodded his head. We had found our commonality, and the mosque project began.

We paid a local architect to design the mosque and local laborers to build it. We purchased all of the materials, the bricks and logs, from local suppliers. Soldiers from the 101st Airborne were assigned to provide security and support. By working together, the infidels and the Pashtoons, we replaced the destroyed mosque and repaired the damage al-Qaeda had done to the community.

Several times a week al-Qaeda fired on our unit. Many of their rockets landed in the farmers' fields around us and even crashed through their roofs, landing in their homes—often without exploding.

Our executive officer, "the Captain," who in real life is a farmer from Idaho, had an idea. He wanted to destroy all of the unexploded rockets in the surrounding fields. So the

Captain went from house to house, asking if the family had unexploded bombs or rockets in their homes or fields and offered to destroy the ordnance to keep the children safe.

The Pashtoon people were so pleased they began coming to the firebase gate, asking for the Captain and showing him where rockets were located, allowing us to destroy the explosives. Soon all of the loose ordnance was destroyed. We had worked together to protect their children.

I found commonality with our interpreter, Abdul. The Captain found it with the fathers of the children around our base, allowing us to accomplish our goal of helping the people of Afghanistan.

I believe that God has placed each of us on this earth with a mission, part of which is to get along with our brothers and sisters, no matter what their creed or culture. In working with people and soldiers all over the world, I have seen time and again that when people find their commonalities, they are more likely to come together and become friends, even under the most stressful conditions.

SERGEANT MAJOR LARRY CHASTON (RET.) is a Vietnam veteran (U.S. Marines) and an Afghanistan veteran (U.S. Army) with over forty years in active duty and National Guard service. In civilian life, he is an engineer, installing robotics. Sergeant Major Chaston and his wife, Judy, have been married for forty-two years. They have six children and seventeen grandchildren.

Just Say No

JESSICA PARIS

I believe in just saying no.

For my sixth birthday, my granddaddy gave me a silver dollar. As big as my palm and strangely weighty, the coin bore the profile of a stern Eisenhower. At that time, 1975, a dollar was twenty times my weekly allowance and would buy me four Milky Way bars, six packs of bubble gum, or twenty Charms Pops. But this dollar was not for spending. It had risen above the pettiness of commerce. This was more like an artifact of history or a piece of public art. So despite my temptations, I said no to Mr. Feeney's candy counter and saved the silver dollar, displaying it on my dresser along with other cherished objects.

This is my first memory of saying no to the razzle-dazzle, lose-ten-pounds-in-ten-days, buy-now-pay-later, you-deserve-a-break-today, just-do-it world we live in. It's not just the media's roar I'm referring to; it's what my family, my friends, sometimes even my inner voice tells me—go ahead, take a break, splurge.

But I have skepticism about pleasure that guides me: I don't believe we satiate our desire by feeding it any more than we do by depriving it. And sometimes deprivation leads to greater satisfaction than indulgence.

Take Thanksgiving. Eating triple portions of turkey and tubers doesn't make me feel gloriously satisfied or thankful. Overcome by gravy, I feel gross. However, occasionally I fast and listen to my stomach's knock, knock, knocking for two days. How chewy, how nutty is that simple cup of brown rice that breaks my fast.

Here are some ways my philosophy currently manifests itself: I say no to sugar before lunch, no to high heels, no to a cell phone, no to artificial sweetener, no to pierced ears, no to bottled water, no to carrying a balance on my credit card.

Sometimes saying no is easier than saying yes—I don't have to say no to thong underwear; it says no to me.

It's not that I'm particularly self-disciplined. The opposite is true. It's because I'm too lazy to rise for a six o'clock jog that I have to at least be able to say "No thanks, I'll walk," when offered a ride home. There are also things I don't resist: books, two-hour phone calls, a six-minute dose of artificial sun to survive Juneau's November.

But when I need it, my strength to say no is bolstered by knowing that every no is a yes to something else. Not owning a car for my first thirty-three years is the reason I have skied to work on the Iditarod trail and why I have walked to work under the pyrotechnics of the morning Northern Lights. And the money I didn't spend on a car allowed me to travel to India, where I rode trains, oxcarts, auto-rickshaws, camels, and even a festooned elephant.

I'm no puritan or prude, martyr or miser. But in a world of such bounty, such opportunity, such Krispy Kremes, choices have to be made. I believe that saying no to some of life's shimmering pleasures buys me a moment of peace and a small sovereign patch where I can pause and ask what it is my heart truly desires. No is not deprivation, it's deliberation. No is not loss, it's freedom.

And my silver dollar? My older brother James stole it to buy Tootsie Rolls and little plastic army men. He believes in saying yes.

JESSICA PARIS is an educator. She lives in Juneau, Alaska, with her husband, two children, and four chickens. They listen to KTOO public radio.

Courage Comes with Practice

THERESA MACPHAIL

I believe that embracing fear produces courage.

After my brother died in an accident, my mother was inconsolable. I was only four years old at the time, but still I understood the seismic shift in my mom's attitude toward safety. Suddenly everything around us was potentially dangerous. Overnight, the world had gone from a playground to a hazardous zone.

I grew up with a lot of restrictions and rules that were meant to protect me. I couldn't walk home from school by myself, even though everyone I knew already did. I couldn't attend pajama parties or go to summer camp, because what if something happened to me?

As I got older, the list of things to fear got longer. My entire life was divided into "things you should avoid" and "things you needed to do in order to have a good, long life." I know my mom was only trying to protect me. She worried about me, because after my brother died I was her only child, and what if something happened to me? What if?

I became a natural worrier. I worry about things like getting cancer, losing my wallet, car accidents, earthquakes, having a brain aneurysm, losing my job, and my plane crashing—disasters big and small, real and imagined.

The funny part is you'd never know it by looking at my life because I'm constantly forcing myself to do the things that frighten or worry me. In fact, I've developed a rule for myself: if it scares me, then I have to do it at least once. I've done lots of things that my mom would have worried about: I've ridden a motorcycle; I've traveled—a lot. In fact, I've lived in China. I've performed stand-up comedy, and I'm planning my second wedding. I still travel to China often, chasing bird flu as a medical anthropologist.

There's something else I don't usually talk about, but it's a cornerstone in my belief: when I was fourteen, my mother died suddenly in a car accident. That loss on top of my brother's unnatural death could have paralyzed me, but at my mom's funeral I remember making a choice. I could either live out the rest of my life trying to be safe or I could be brave enough to live out a fulfilling, exciting, and yes, sometimes dangerous life.

I worry that I may have betrayed my mother by writing about her in this light, but she has been a driving force in my life and, in the end, I think she would have been proud of me. Courage isn't a natural attribute of human beings. I believe that we have to practice being courageous; using courage is like developing a muscle. The more often I do things that scare me or that make me uncomfortable, the more I realize that I can do a lot more than I originally thought I could do.

Even though I inherited my mother's cautious nature, I've also come to believe that fear can be a good thing, if we face it. Believing that has made my world a less scary place.

THERESA MACPHAIL is a medical anthropologist at the University of California, Berkeley. A writer and former reporter, she authored *The Eye of the Virus*, a fictional account of a bird flu pandemic, and is currently at work on a nonfiction book on the 2009 H1N1 pandemic. Ms. MacPhail lives in Berkeley with her husband and two cats.

Adapting to the Possibilities of Life

DONALD L. ROSENSTEIN, M.D.

I believe in adaptation—that is, the same stimulus does not invariably elicit the same response over time.

The first time I saw my son flap his arms, I nearly threw up.

My son Koby was two at the time, and he and my wife and I were at an evening luau in Hawaii. Dancers emerged from the dark, twirling torches to loud, rhythmic drumbeats. I thought it was exciting, and so did Koby. He began to flap his arms—slowly, at first, and then with an intensity that mirrored the movement of the dancers.

In an instant, I was overwhelmed. I knew just enough about arm flapping to know that it was characteristic of autism. I was confused, panicked, and strangely preoccupied with the fear that I would never play tennis with my son as I had with my father. That one movement took on an immediate, powerful, and symbolic meaning: something was terribly wrong with my boy.

Koby is sixteen years old now. He lost his language skills, developed epilepsy, and has struggled profoundly. We've all struggled, including Koby's little sister, Emma. But we've also adapted. Koby still flaps his arms, and he's got the thick, muscular upper body one would expect after fourteen years of isometric exercise. He's a sweet and beautiful boy, and together we've been on a journey into frightening and unknown territory. Like any fellow travelers, we've learned from each other and grown.

Koby's arm flapping means something different to me now. It means that he's interested, tuned in, and present in the moment.

That Koby has autism is old news at this point. We've grieved, survived, and adapted. We've learned to be more patient, to celebrate more modest victories, and to connect with Koby whenever and however we can. Now, when Koby flaps, I'm happy for him and what it means about his engagement, not sickened by what it might mean for his and our futures.

Same stimulus, different response.

I believe that this lesson in adaptation has been one of Koby's greatest gifts to me, to our whole family. I've seen it as Emma's embarrassment over her brother's condition has faded and been replaced with compassion for those who struggle. And I've seen the influence of Koby's lesson in my own work, helping patients cope with illness and tragedy in their lives—like my patient who can finally celebrate her father's memory after years of debilitating grief that came with every anniversary of his death.

Last summer, Koby had a delirious romp in the ocean alongside Emma. Koby flapped his arms wildly in anticipation of each coming wave. Not quite the family beach day we had once envisioned, but a spectacular moment nonetheless.

Old heartbreak, new appreciation.

I believe that "reframing a problem" can help to overcome it. But adaptation is not the same as becoming tolerant of or inured to something. Adaptation allows for creative possibilities. Koby has adapted to us and we to him, and through this process our family has discovered deep and meaningful connections with each other—connections we never thought possible.

As director of the Comprehensive Cancer Support Program, DR. DONALD ROSENSTEIN specializes in psychiatric care of patients with cancer. He is also on the board of KEEN—Kids Enjoy Exercise Now—a national recreation program for disabled youth. Dr. Rosenstein and his family live in Chapel Hill, North Carolina.

Why Are We Here?

DALE LONG

Why are we here? This is a timeless question that expresses humanity's fundamental desire to understand our collective existence and value.

On a more personal level, why am I here? Many other people seem to have a pretty clear opinion of why I'm here. My wife believes I'm here to take out the garbage, help the children with their homework, and rub her feet. My boss believes I'm here to do my job and do it well. The person in the car behind me this morning looked as if she believed I was there to make her late.

However, while living up to everyone else's expectations may give our existence purpose of a sort, it's not the same as figuring out our own answer about why we, personally, are here. It took a while, but I believe I found at least part of my answer a few years ago.

I remember clearly the first time I had a real sense of my place in the universe. I was forty-two years old and had just bought our family a telescope. The astronomy software that came with the telescope said we'd be able to see Saturn that same night. I'd never seen a planet with my own eyes before, just pictures. We located a bright dot in the sky where Saturn was supposed to be and lined up the telescope. Saturn came into focus, looking like a tiny, round ball suspended inside a small, flat washer.

As I stepped back from the telescope to let the children have a look, I realized my whole view of the universe had just changed dramatically. On an intellectual level, I had always known that the twinkling lights in the sky were stars and planets. But at some primal level I had never really believed they were anything but pinholes in the roof of the world. Now, I could not deny it any longer. Planets, stars, and galaxies were real. The universe stretches to as close to infinity as mankind will ever comprehend. I got to savor the moment for all of five seconds until the children bumped the telescope and I had to line it up for them again.

I believe I understand why scientists like Copernicus and Galileo risked imprisonment and death for reporting the results of their astronomical discoveries, and it was for the same reasons that prophets like Buddha, Moses, Jesus, and Muhammad risked imprisonment and death for preaching their faith: they had discovered something wonderful and wanted to expand human understanding of our place in creation.

Many people are comfortable with their belief of where they are in the universe, of course, and will resist any attempt to dislodge their current view of reality, either spiritually or scientifically. But I believe mankind will only continue to make progress by seeking out and embracing new knowledge, wisdom, and insights into both science and spirit in tandem. Science without spirituality is cold and sterile; spirituality without science is merely wishful thinking.

Why are we here? Maybe it's simply to find a balance between what we believe and what we perceive as we journey through life. I believe I can live with that answer.

DALE LONG lives in South Burlington, Vermont, with his awesome wife and two wonderful children. He is a former professional musician, retired military officer, government technocrat, amateur astronomer, Aikido black belt, teacher, writer, and storyteller who believes that specialization is for insects, not people.

A Drive to Achieve the Extraordinary

JULIET FRERKING

I believe in the challenge to accomplish something out of the ordinary. I have to confess I acquired this belief from the book *Guinness World Records.* That book showed me the value of equal opportunity and competition. It proved to me, early on, that I could rise above anonymity and achieve remarkable things.

When I was nine, I used to huddle in the back of the library with my friend Leanne, and we'd turn the 1991 edition of the *Guinness World Records* book pages with purple hands sticky from raspberry Laffy Taffy. Reassured by Mrs. Balanoff, our third grade teacher, that we could be anything when we grew up, we felt challenged by 320 pages of incredible feats. And so with the obsessive focus of nine-year-olds, we assumed the daily task of finding our place in the universe.

The *Guinness World Records* taught me to believe in the accessibility of the improbable. I was captured by the little bit of fame conferred by inclusion in that book: the fastest, the longest, the widest, the most—whatever you can imagine. It opened up the possibilities of what I might be able to do.

I was attracted to the lure of the unusual. How long would it take to grow my fingernails to beat a record for a total of fourteen feet, six inches? I bet our teachers never thought the equation $d = rt$ would be used to figure that one out, or that we would be tempted to research everything about Namibia because it was home to the world's fastest caterpillar. Leanne settled on holding her breath for the longest time, and I decided to make the world's largest cookie. Thus, Leanne joined the swim team, and I gained ten pounds.

The *Guinness World Records* taught me tenacity and perseverance and, more important, the desire to do something unexpected. So many people in the book were mocked by family and friends for what they were doing, yet they did it. I see them as success stories—normal people who did something extraordinary.

In college, before September 11, I decided to study Arabic. I am not Muslim or of Arab decent; I am a Southern Baptist girl from Texas. Enticed by the sounds of elongated alifs and lams, I fell in love with the complexity of the language and the beauty of its slanting script. After graduation, to put my skills to use, I moved to Cairo and then to Tunisia, where I just finished working with divorced women.

I am not saving the world, I am not the best at what I do, but I am only twenty-four—there's still time. The *Guinness World Records* helped give me a new perspective on the impossible and instilled in me the desire to try something unconventional. I believe in making the implausible a reality, and I hope to someday break a few records myself.

JULIET FRERKING graduated from Stanford University in 2005 with honors in international relations and a minor in Arabic language. In 2008 she conducted research in Tunisia under a Fulbright Fellowship. Ms. Frerking currently lives in New York City.

Inviting the World to Dinner

JIM HAYNES

Every week for the past thirty years I have hosted a Sunday dinner in my home in Paris. People, including total strangers, call or e-mail to book a spot. I hold the salon in my atelier, which used to be a sculpture studio. The first fifty or sixty people who call may come—twice that many when the weather is nice and we can overflow into the garden.

Every Sunday a different friend prepares a feast. Last week it was a philosophy student from Lisbon, and next week a dear friend from London will cook.

People from all corners of the world come to break bread together, to meet, to talk, to connect, and often to become friends. All ages, nationalities, races, and professions gather here, and since there is no organized seating, the opportunity for mingling couldn't be better. I love the randomness.

I believe in introducing people to people.

I have a good memory, so each week I make a point to remember everyone's name on the guest list and where they're from and what they do so I can introduce them to one another, effortlessly. If I had my way, I would introduce everyone in the whole world to one another.

People are the most important thing in my life. Many travelers go to see things like the Tower of London, the Statue of Liberty, the Eiffel Tower, and so on. I travel to see friends, even—or especially—those I've never met.

In the late 1980s, I edited a series of guidebooks to nine Eastern European countries and Russia. There were no sights to see, no shops or museum to visit; instead, each book contained about a thousand short biographies of people who would be willing to welcome travelers in their cities. Hundreds of friendships evolved from these encounters, including marriages and babies, too.

The same can be said for my Sunday salon. At a recent dinner a six-year-old girl from Bosnia spent the entire evening glued to an eight-year-old boy from Estonia. Their parents were surprised, and pleased, by this immediate friendship.

There is always a collection of people from all over the globe. Most of them speak English, at least as a second language. Recently a dinner featured a typical mix: a Dutch political cartoonist, a beautiful painter from Norway, a truck driver from Arizona, a bookseller from Atlanta, a newspaper editor from Sydney, students from all over, and traveling retirees.

I have long believed that it is unnecessary to understand others, individuals, or nationalities; one must, at the very least, simply tolerate others. Tolerance can lead to respect and, finally, to love. No one can ever really understand anyone else, but you can love them or at least accept them.

Like Tom Paine, I am a world citizen. All human history is mine. My roots cover the earth.

I believe we should know each other. After all, our lives are all connected.

Okay, now come and dine.

JIM HAYNES was born in Louisiana, spent his teens in Venezuela, attended boarding school in Atlanta and university in Louisiana, then served in the military in Scotland. He created a bookshop and the Traverse Theatre in Edinburgh and the Arts Laboratory Mixed Media Centre in London. He also cofounded a newspaper in London and another in Amsterdam. After teaching sexual politics and media studies at the University of Paris 8 for thirty years, Mr. Haynes retired in 1999. Since colaunching the Sunday dinners in the mid-1970s, some 140,000 people from all corners of the world have dined with Mr. Haynes.

Finding the Flexibility to Survive

BRIGHTON EARLEY

Every Friday night the cashier at the Chevron gas station food mart on Eagle Rock Boulevard and Avenue 40 offers us a discount on all of the leftover apples and bananas. To ensure the best selection possible, my mother and I pile into our twenty-year-old car and pull up to the food mart at five p.m. on the dot, ready to get our share of slightly overripe fruits.

Before the times of the Chevron food mart, there were the times of the calculator. My mother would carefully prop it up in the cart's child seat and frown as she entered each price. Since the first days of the calculator's appearance, the worry lines on my mother's face have only grown deeper. Today, they are a permanent fixture.

Chevron shopping started like this: One day my mother suddenly realized that she had maxed out almost every credit card, and we needed groceries for the week. The only credit card she hadn't maxed out was the Chevron card, and the station on Eagle Rock Boulevard has a pretty big mart attached to it.

Since our first visit there, I've learned to believe in flexibility. In my life, it has become necessary to bend the idea of grocery shopping. My mother and I can no longer shop at real grocery stores, but we still get the necessities.

Grocery shopping at Chevron has its drawbacks. The worst is when we have so many items that it takes the checker what seems like hours to ring up everything. A line of anxious customers forms behind us. It's that line that hurts the most—the way they look at us. My mother never notices—or maybe she pretends not to.

I never need to be asked to help the checker bag all of the items. No one wants to get out of there faster than I do. I'm embarrassed to shop there, and I'm deathly afraid of running into someone I know. I once expressed my fear of being seen shopping at Chevron to my mother, and her eyes shone with disappointment. I know that I hurt her feelings when I try to evade our weekly shopping trips.

And that is why I hold on to the idea of flexibility so tightly. I believe that being flexible keeps me going—keeps me from being ashamed of the way my family is different from other families. Whenever I feel the heat rise to my face, I remind myself that grocery shopping at a gas station is just a twist on the normal kind of grocery shopping. I remind myself that we won't always have to shop at Chevron—that just because at this point in my life I am struggling does not mean that I will always struggle. My belief in flexibility helps me get through the difficult times, because I know that no matter what happens, my mother and I will always figure out a way to survive.

BRIGHTON EARLEY will graduate from the University of California, Berkeley, with a B.A. in English in May 2012. She plans to pursue a graduate degree in English or creative writing so she can teach at the college level. Ms. Earley continues to enjoy writing essays of all kinds, and for her fiction writing, she recently received a Pushcart Prize nomination.

The Act of Giving Thanks

MICHELLE LEE

I believe in meaningful expressions of gratitude. More specifically, I believe in the power of the well-written thank-you letter.

My sister and I were taught at a very early age to write thank-you letters for birthday and Christmas gifts. We carefully copied addresses from our mom's address book into our own pretty little books, and a new box of stationery was always among my gifts wrapped under the tree. We wrote our letters on December 26. At the latest. Every year. It was an important ritual in our home, and it has turned me into an avid thank-you-letter writer as an adult.

I still send a great deal of personal mail, and I am entirely smitten with all of the trappings of letter writing: unique stamps, beautiful stationery, fountain pens. I feel an incredible rush of satisfaction sticking a stamp on a carefully penned thank-you letter and sending it off in the mail.

Nearly every Monday morning I sit down with my favorite pen and write a few thank-yous. I write them for parties I attend, dinners I'm fed, or just to thank a friend for listening. It is one of the highlights of my week.

Several years ago I even sent my mom a thank-you letter to thank her for teaching me to count my blessings on paper. Sending letters of thanks out into the world has made me more appreciative of the tremendous love, support, and kindness I receive daily.

My father died when I was twenty-seven. Even then, I found comfort in writing letters of thanks for the many gifts of words I received. At a time when all I wanted to do was retreat into my own grief, the act of giving thanks forced me to stay connected to the world and to the lives of the living.

And while it may seem trivial, my belief in well-written thank-you letters has secured my popularity. Since real thank-you letters are woefully few and far between, my social graces are considered a charming eccentricity, and my friends and family always seem genuinely moved by my efforts.

I was a middle school English teacher, and as I told my students, good manners are the cornerstone of a quality community. I believe that expressions of gratitude like thank-you letters keep me going. I am more motivated to do kind things for others when I feel appreciated, and I feel that I perpetuate kindness and generosity by genuinely expressing my thanks.

What many people consider to be a dreadful chore has become one of my favorite pastimes. So simple, the thank-you letter, but so powerful.

MICHELLE LEE is a writer, editor, and former middle school English teacher from Longmont, Colorado. When not playing around with words, she loves to cook, spend time with her two children, play cribbage with her husband, and tackle the *New York Times* crossword puzzle.

Sally's Monday

PATRICIA JAMES

I believe in showing up. My mother avoided visiting her best friend, my godmother, as she died of lung cancer because she didn't know what to do or say. Even when Berdelle's family called to say it wouldn't be long, Mom couldn't go. She never said good-bye.

A few years later Mom died of Lou Gehrig's disease. In the days surrounding her death, our small Minnesota town transformed itself into an ark that kept our family afloat. For weeks, people did the simplest things: vacuumed, brought food, drank coffee with my father, and mowed the lawn. It all mattered.

In 2003, my dear friend, Sally, was diagnosed with lung cancer. Like Berdelle, she was a nonsmoker. Like my mom, I didn't know what to do or say. I did a flurry of research to learn all there was to know about non-small-cell carcinoma and considered training to become a hospice volunteer. Then my life partner reminded me to do what I already knew how to do: show up.

A group of Sally's friends—she called us the Divas—made sure that someone was with her every day of the week. I was Sally's Monday. Our days at the cancer center were filled with talking, knitting, and hilarity that often involved medical staff and other patients.

Back home, Sally had a list of projects. We sorted through scary accumulations of photographs, craft projects, cosmetics, old purses, wallpaper, stationery, scarves, flowerpots, books, mismatched linens, and schmaltzy knickknacks stashed in closets and cabinets. We went to the gym and cheered when Sally sustained one mile an hour on the treadmill for ten minutes. One day we traded in her car for a smaller model that everyone else drove after the cancer was in her brain. We went to the mall to buy pajamas for her husband's Christmas present. We browsed through her favorite dollar store, dropped off the latest pictures of her granddaughter Emerson to be developed, took drives in the country so she could take pictures on her new camera phone, promising we'd figure out how to download them someday. Sometimes we sat in her living room and folded laundry.

Each visit ended with a game of freestyle Scrabble for which we made new rules as needed. I knew the end was near when Sally couldn't organize her letters to be right side up and didn't remember we could make a rule allowing upside-down words.

Sally died on December 27, 2005. We hadn't had any deep conversations about dying and death—those were reserved for her beloved husband and children. With her friends, she was as much herself as she could be, and that's what she wanted. She needed her friends to show up and do the simplest things. And we did.

PATRICIA JAMES was born and raised in Northfield, Minnesota, and now lives outside of Philadelphia. She is the education director at the Pennsylvania Horticultural Society. A longtime member of the Rittenhouse Writers Group, Ms. James has just completed her first novel.

If You Don't Do It, Who Will?

JODI WEBB

My mom has always been involved, whether it was the church, the school, the team, or the community. And where my mom volunteered, other family members often followed. I remember her comment whenever I protested about a volunteer activity she recruited me for. "It's for the church" or "It's for the school."

When we were growing up my mom focused most of her energy, and the family's, on those organizations because they relied on volunteers to survive. My brother ran the sound equipment for the school's annual Christmas play, my dad made bean soup for the church's summer festival,

I spent a few sweltering days reorganizing the elementary school library at the end of each school year. How could anyone dare to refuse? Each demand was accompanied by that unspoken question, "If you don't do it, who will?"

For my mother, volunteering was as natural as breathing or cleaning out the closets each spring. If it needed to be done and you were capable of doing it, you did it. I like to think of our volunteering as a family trait, like blue eyes or bossiness (both of which run in the family). My grandmother, my mother, and I were all raised in the same small town populated mostly by coal miners. The residents didn't have much money, but they always had a willingness to help. When my grandparents were young, the town didn't have a church, so the miners, after spending twelve hours a day underground, built one. It's just our nature in this town.

Now as an adult and mother of three children, I have raised my hand at more meetings than I care to count, because that unspoken truth was echoing inside me. As a Girl Scout leader, I spent my Thursday evenings with sixteen energetic Brownies. As a lunchtime recruiter, I begged dozens of parents to become cafeteria helpers. I baked dozens of cookies to raise money for the school gardening club. If I didn't do it, who would?

That little question has also encouraged me to take action in other aspects of my life when I would have preferred to just stay in bed. If I don't slosh through the rain puddles to vote out an ineffective politician, who will? If I don't protect my health by cutting fat, adding calcium, and exercising, who will? If I don't turn off TV programs that are inappropriate for my children, who will?

Sometimes the responsibility that comes with that question seems overwhelming. Responsibility for yourself, your family, your community, your government, your environment. How freeing it would be to turn the obligations of life over to that anonymous group we all love to rely on: "them." Let "them" worry about endangered whales. Let "them" pick up roadside trash. Let "them" serve on the school board. Let "them" collect tickets at a fund-raiser. But that isn't what my mother taught me. I could do it. I believe I should do it.

After all, if I don't, who will?

JODI WEBB is a writer from Pottsville, Pennsylvania. Her three children enjoy the quirk that makes her bake cookies when she has writer's block. Ms. Webb's latest volunteer project is agreeing to take charge of the Box Tops for Education/Labels for Education program at her son's elementary school.

Here Comes (the Real)
Santa Claus

BECKY SUN

I believe in Santa Claus. No, I didn't always believe, but nine years ago, on Christmas Eve, he knocked on my front door and handed me a stocking filled with candy and toys.

Unlike the majority of my friends, I wasn't introduced to the jolly guy until second grade. My family emigrated from Taiwan to a small town in central Georgia, where my dad got a visa for his family and a job doctoring inmates at a nearby penitentiary. I had just learned English, and from what little I could gather from my classmates, there was this guy who would come down one's chimney and put toys in one's stocking on Christmas Eve! What a great country,

I thought. After I looked up *stocking* in my Chinese-English dictionary, I knew what I had to do.

On that fateful night, after everyone went to bed, I took my longest, cleanest knee sock and attached it to a nail already on the mantel. Obviously, the previous owners of this house were no strangers to this Santa character. Unfortunately, my parents were.

I woke up before everyone else on Christmas Day and ran to the fireplace. To make a sob story short, I was hit with the reality of a flaccid sock and the biggest lie ever told. I indulged in a few tears, quickly took down the sock, and stuffed it in the back of a drawer. Santa was dead.

Every December since then, the topic of Christmas memories would inevitably come up, and I would regale my friends with my poor-little-me story. I had to make it as wry as possible, or else I would cry.

How could I know that Santa was just late? Nine years ago, on Christmas Eve, an older man with a white beard and a red cap knocked on my front door. He said, "I've been looking for you for twenty-five years." He handed me a bulging red stocking, winked, and left. On top of the stocking was a card. It read: "For Becky—I may have missed you in the second grade, but you've always lived in my heart. Santa."

Through tear-blurred eyes, I recognized the curlicue handwriting of Jill, a friend I had met just two months before. I later discovered that the older man was her father. Jill had seen the hurt little girl underneath the jaded thirty-something woman and decided to do something about it.

So now I believe that Santa is real. I don't mean the twinkle-eyed elf of children's mythology or the creation of American holiday marketers. Those Santas annoy and sadden me. I believe in the Santa Claus that dwells inside good and thoughtful people. This Santa does not return to the North Pole after a twenty-four-hour delivery frenzy but lives each day purposefully, really listens to friends, and then plans deliberate acts of kindness.

BECKY SUN is a senior editor for Iconoculture, a consumer insights company. She lives in Minneapolis with her husband and three children, whose stockings are filled with care every Christmas Eve.

APPENDIX

How to Write Your Own
This I Believe Essay

We invite you to contribute to this project by writing and submitting your own statement of personal belief. We understand how challenging this is—it requires such intimacy that you may find it difficult to begin. To guide you through this process, we offer these suggestions:

Tell a story. Be specific. Take your belief out of the ether and ground it in the events of your life. Your story need not be heartwarming or gut-wrenching—it can even be funny—but it should be real. Consider moments when your belief was formed, tested, or changed. Make sure your story ties to the essence of your daily life philosophy and to the shaping of your beliefs.

Be brief. Your statement should be between 350 and 500 words. The shorter length forces you to focus on the belief that is central to your life.

Name your belief. If you can't name it in a sentence or two, your essay might not be about belief. Rather than writing a list, consider focusing on one core belief.

Be positive. Say what you *do* believe, not what you *don't* believe. Avoid statements of religious dogma, preaching, or editorializing.

Be personal. Make your essay about you; speak in the first person. Try reading your essay aloud to yourself several times, and each time edit it and simplify it until you find the words, tone, and story that truly echo your belief and the way you speak.

Please submit your completed essay to the *This I Believe* project by visiting the website, www.thisibelieve.org. We are eager for your contribution.

ACKNOWLEDGMENTS

First and foremost, we offer our deepest gratitude to the essayists who contributed their work to this book. We honor their willingness to express the things that matter most and to share their stories in this collection.

In reviving *This I Believe*, we are forever grateful to Casey Murrow, Keith Wheelock, and Margot Wheelock Schlegel, the children of *This I Believe* creators Edward R. Murrow and Ward Wheelock. Our project continues to be guided by Edward R. Murrow and his team, which preceded us in the 1950s: Gladys Chang Hardy, Reny Hill, Donald J. Merwin, Edward P. Morgan, Raymond Swing, and Ward Wheelock.

Very special thanks go to Atlantic Public Media, Inc., in Woods Hole, Massachusetts, where many of these essays were first reviewed. Several essays in this collection were originally broadcast on NPR, and we are thankful to Jay Allison and Viki Merrick for their contribution in editing and producing these essays: "The Power of Hello," "The Art of Being a Neighbor," "A Kind and Generous Heart," "Caring Makes Us Human," "A Priceless Lesson in Humility," "Accomplishing Big Things in Small Pieces," "Deciding to Live," "Walking in the Light," "Listening Is Powerful Medicine," "Our Vulnerability Is Our Strength," "A Taste of Success," "Seeing with the Heart," "To Hear Your Inner Voice," "Courage Comes with Practice," "Adapting to the Possibilities of Life," "A Drive to Achieve the Extraordinary," "Inviting the World to Dinner," and "Finding the Flexibility to Survive." We also appreciate the production assistance provided by Posey Gruener.

Our sincerest thanks to Laura Coons for expert editorial assistance. Her insights and organization were of immense help in bringing this book to life.

We are truly and deeply grateful for our This I Believe, Inc., board of directors, who give their time and talents to strengthening our organization. Thank you to Marty Bollinger, John Y. Brown III, Jerry Howe, David Langstaff, Lynn Amato Madonna, and Declan Murphy.

Our current on-air homes are *The Bob Edwards Show* on Sirius XM Satellite Radio and *Bob Edwards Weekend* on

Public Radio International. Our heartfelt thanks go to Bob Edwards and his wonderful staff: Steve Lickteig, Geoffrey Redick, Ed McNulty, Ariana Pekary, Shelley Tillman, Dan Bloom, Andy Kubis, Chad Campbell, and Cristy Meiners. At Sirius XM, we thank Jeremy Coleman, Frank Raphael, and Kevin Straley.

We also want to express our gratitude to everyone at NPR, which aired our radio series for the first four years, especially Jay Kernis, Stacey Foxwell, and Robert Spier, who were passionate and steadfast supporters.

The comprehensive website for *This I Believe* (thisibelieve .org) was built by Dennis Whiteman at Fastpipe Media, Inc., and was designed by the folks at LeapFrog Interactive with help from Chris Enander of TBD Design. Our iPhone app was cocreated by Dennis along with Wayne Walrath at Acme Technologies.

The creation of this book was immeasurably aided by our agent, Andrew Blauner, of Blauner Books Literary Agency. We are so fortunate to continue to have his able services and his unwavering support.

Our publisher, John Wiley & Sons, has been tremendously supportive of our recent publishing activities. We are deeply indebted to editor Hana Lane and her entire team for their passion and professionalism. We are deeply grateful especially for the skills and support of Ellen Wright, Lisa Burstiner, Matt Smollon, Mike Onorato, and Laura Cusack.

And, finally, we thank the thousands of individuals who have accepted our invitation to write and to share their own personal statements of belief. This book contains but a fraction of the many thoughtful and inspiring essays that have been submitted to our project, and we are grateful for them all. We invite you to join this group by writing your own *This I Believe* essay and submitting it to us via our website, thisibelieve.org. You will find instructions in the appendix of this book on how to do so.